The Mystery Of The Trinity Revealed

The Mystery Of The Trinity Revealed

Unveiling the Triune God

T. R. Bosse

Dove & Word Publishing

The Mystery of the Trinity Revealed;
Copyright © (2017) by T.R. Bosse

All Rights Reserved. – No part of this book may be reproduced, stored in a retrieval system or transmitted in any form or by any means–electronic, mechanical, photocopying, recording, or otherwise without prior written permission from the publisher. The only exception is brief quotations in printed reviews.

All Scripture quotations are from the Authorized King James Version of the Bible. Specific Scripture pronouns attributed to the Godhead are capitalized to establish a contrast between the fundamental nature of mortal man and the deified nature ascribed to God.

(*Hardback-2019*)
ISBN: 978-0-9723974-3-8
Revised Edition (2021)

© Cover design by RL Sather

Published by:

Dove & Word Publishing
PO Box 47
Union, KY 41091

PRINTED IN THE UNITED STATES OF AMERICA

Contents

Introduction..vii
1. Objective and Design...............................1
2. Purpose and History................................9
3. The Creation of Man..............................17
4. Examining Spiritual Issues....................25
5. The Totality of Man...............................33
6. The Blood..39
7. Satan's Ultimate Intent..........................47
8. The Virgin Birth....................................53
9. Jesus–The Second Adam......................61
10. What the Cross Fulfilled......................69
11. The Born-again Experience.................73
12. Messiah and Prophecies......................79
13. Issues Surrounding the Trinity............85
14. The Humanity of Christ.......................93
15. The Holy Spirit..................................101
16. Declarations of His Deity..................105
17. The Revelation of the Trinity............109
(Part 1 - The Covenants)
18. The Revelation of the Trinity............115
(Part 2 - The seed of Abraham and David)
19. The Revelation of the Trinity............121
(Part 3 - The Substance of the Pure Seed)
20. The Final Analysis.............................131

Introduction

Ever since the 1st Century, men have attempted to comprehend the Trinity. Even the apostles who wrote the New Testament did not detail the Virgin Birth or the Triune God. Lacking the ability to understand this elusive Christian doctrine has prompted many theologians to render it a mystery. However, while that was the case as little as 100 years ago, things have changed. Today's technology is beyond the imagination of all past societies. The 12th chapter of Daniel mentions clearly that in the last days, knowledge shall increase. Though it seems those specifics apply only to the secular world, its relevance for the Bible is invaluable.

Many technical advances have affected the Word of God. One of the most notable passages concerns the two witnesses in (Revelation 11:9). From the biblical context, we find that the whole world would see them lying in the streets of Jerusalem. However, before the 20th Century, no one could realize how that would be possible. Today with television, cell phones, and satellites, the answer is obvious.

The Bible also alludes to inventions such as the automobile, airplanes, computers, and modern military weaponry. So too, with the Trinity, such things as DNA, blood analysis, ultrasound, instruments, probes, and other apparatus' allow us to understand the human anatomy as never before. Yet, they also help us explain the Virgin Birth, the Blood of Jesus, the sin-nature, and a host of other hidden-in-plain-sight biblical facts.

This book's basis transpired from a revelation received in December 1999, two weeks before the new millennium. Research and more revelations to find realistic answers continued for several years until it yielded Trinity's completed picture. The results confirmed that the Trinity was never a mystery, but God's timing prevented the revelation until the wake of today's advanced knowledge.

The Mystery of the Trinity Revealed contains an urgent revelation for Christians and an eye-opening disclosure for society. May this book illuminate your heart as you receive this critical message hidden from ages past but now revealed to us in these last days.

T.R. Bosse

Chapter 1
Objective and Design

Who is God? You might expect many different answers from the numerous religions in the world. Some look up to the sun, moon, and stars; others reverence wooden and concrete statues. However, of those various belief systems, only two (Judaism and Christianity) worship the God of the Bible, and only one (Christianity) believes in the Trinity. Although the Bible contains many expressions attributed to God, a statement from the book of Deuteronomy offers something seemingly contradictory in our objective to reveal the Trinity. The passage presents the following quote by Moses, "Hear, O Israel: The Lord our God is one Lord." Over the years, this declaration has kept many from accepting the Trinity as truth. One reason for the unbelief centers on a New Testament passage where Jesus proclaimed that He and His Father are One (John 10:30). When we compare Jesus' proclamation in contrast to what Moses declared, a puzzling question confronts us, "How can *two* Gods be one Lord?" Yet, adding even more disparity to the episode, another entity enters the scene, namely God the Holy Ghost. Now the question becomes, "How can *three* Gods be one Lord?"

An assortment of other questions has made the Trinity doctrine one of the most controversial yet least understood topics ever to confront humanity. Many world belief systems teach their followers that the Trinity is a mystery that expresses three Gods. However, society is not alone in regarding it as a mystery because most Christians do as well. Scholars and theologians sought to realize this puzzling doctrine throughout the ages, but to no avail. What prevented them from finding factual answers? Did God purposely keep this biblical truth hidden from us? Should such an essential Christian doctrine forever carry a stigma that makes it an everlasting secret, or was the Trinity ever a real mystery after all?

You shall find in this study that the mystification behind the Trinity hinged on the fact that throughout history, God had never revealed it to anyone until these last days. We shall cover that issue later, but for now, let us establish the view most people currently hold.

The following is a short assessment of how the legendary account of Saint Patrick dealt with the issue. In an attempt to project the Trinity to an outdoor church gathering, Patrick struggled for answers and found himself at a loss for words. Suddenly, looking down, something within the meadow caught his eye. Therein, he spotted a shamrock. He picked it up and proceeded to give this comparison. The three leaves symbolized the Father, the Son, and the Holy Ghost. The stem of the shamrock represented the one, God. Patrick's speculation seemed reasonable considering his available choices. However, it provided little insight or substance to answer the many questions designed to put the so-called mystery to rest.

More recently, present-day ministers have endeavored to explain the Trinity by attempting other versions of analogies. One preacher offered this example, "The best way to explain the Trinity is to compare it to an egg, whereas the shell signifies God the Father, the yoke represents God the Son, and the white depicts God the Holy Ghost." In a separate setting, another clergy member donated a different version comparing the Trinity to the three stages of water. He illustrated the liquid as the Father, ice represented the Son, and steam symbolized the Holy Ghost.

These illustrations represent a small sampling of the many examples attempting to explain the Trinity. Could analogies be the only means of disclosure? These ideas seem very reasonable, especially to those who believe the Trinity will forever remain a mystery. As these examples suggest, and after centuries of seeking answers, most theologians and scholars share a collective view that the Trinity is an inconceivable mystery. Thus, if most Church leaders have reached this conclusion, it would seem logical for the layperson to hold the same opinion.

Objective and Design

The purpose of this book is to uncover all the issues that kept the Trinity a mystery over the years and provide answers that will leave no doubt to its authenticity. Questions used in the past to discredit the doctrine will become a thing of the past. Perhaps the most problematic issue most people do not consider is the systematic processes of the Bible. Those techniques explain how God works to convey His Word to us in the past, present, and future times. Every happening in the Bible allows the next event's progression to occur in the order God so designed for it to take place. For example, the Creation in Genesis would not fit in Revelation. The same holds for placing the New Testament before the Old. In like manner, the reason the early Church fathers were unable to unveil the Trinity is evident. Today's vast wealth of knowledge was not available back then. However, discoveries within our modern health fields disclose several essential details designed to aid in clearing up Trinity's mystery.

Keep in mind, everything occurs within God's time frame and not that He kept any secrets from us. The Bible did not hide the Trinity because every Scripture verse is open for our eyes to see. Yet, God did provide for its disclosure to fit where He always chooses to disclose things to us—in His perfect timing.

Reasoning:
The Trinity is the central teaching of Christianity. If Jesus were not God in the flesh, Christians would worship an imperfect mortal. As a mere man, Jesus would originate from Adam and become subject to sin. If He were an angel or another type of being, he would not qualify as the deliverer to redeem humanity from its sins. Nevertheless, many cannot conceive of a God who declared Himself as the One God, became human, lived on earth, and died as a man. Therefore, some have submitted seemingly valid arguments to reject the Trinity. One popular stance concerns the omission of the word Trinity from the Bible. Another view challenges the exclusion of Jesus' name in the Old Testament. Even others point out that the word Trinity did not exist until years after Christ was on earth. One of the more favored allegations contends that Scripture writings contain inaccuracies. While the first such charges may be correct, we find that the Bible does not contain contradictions or errors.

Trinity and Life:

The word Trinity generally conjures up a portrait of God and His Godhead. However, another image must also share the limelight, and it regards the subject matter called life. On that basis, God laid out His design for humanity. It is also why many ask numerous questions concerning their purpose in life and why they exist.

Predestination in the Bible refers to God's foreknowledge of how each person would choose the outcome for their existence in life through their own free will. Therefore, God already knows the destiny you and I will select during our time on earth. Knowing that choice, God carefully preordained each life to fit within a far-reaching blueprint of His long-range objective. Thus, He designated every individual to exist at the right time and place in history. The following passage provides insight into this course of action:

- "And (God) hath made of one blood (Adam) all nations of men for to dwell on all the face of the earth, and hath determined the times before appointed, and the bounds of their habitation." **(Acts 17:26)**

Many individuals view the Trinity using definitions or explanations rather than the perspective called life. The definition viewpoint declares that there is one Lord God, who manifests Himself in three separate, but distinct entities: the Father, the Son, and the Holy Ghost. Since both Jesus and the Holy Ghost derive from the Father and not of or from themselves, provide further verification, there is only one God and not three as some maintain.

Verified Throughout:

Even though the Old Testament does not mention the word Trinity or the name Jesus outright, many passages allude to them in one way or another. Could it be a coincidence that the first verse of the Bible (Genesis 1:1) indicates the Father? The next verse discovers the Spirit (Holy Ghost), and we find the Son (Jesus) in the third verse. Meanwhile, verse 26 suggests the complete Godhead, and Genesis 3:15 points to the first coming of Jesus. Then again, verse 3:22 depicts another reference to the Godhead.

We find other indications of the Godhead, particularly the Son, sprinkled throughout the Old Testament without mentioning Jesus or the word Trinity. However, it is not by accident that those two expressions are nonexistent in the Old Testament. The following New Testament passage shows the purpose of their omission:

- "But we speak the wisdom of God in a mystery, even the hidden wisdom, which God ordained before the world unto our glory: Which none of the princes of this world knew: for had they known it they would **not** have crucified the Lord of glory." **(1 Corinthians 2:7)**

This verse displays a prime reason why the Old Testament did not mention Jesus' name. God ordained a mystery before the world *began*. The princes of this world refer to Satan and his hordes, which is a clear indication that the ones who instituted the crucifixion were the demonic forces of this world. Thus, the devil would have recognized Jesus' purpose in the New Testament by seeing His name mentioned in the Old Testament. If the devil knew of God's plan to send Jesus to earth to die for the world's sins, the crucifixion would not have happened. That would also mean no redemption for humanity.

The epistle of Romans also suggests another reason for omitting the words Jesus and the Trinity. It attests that God purposely kept these things secret for disclosure in the time it was preordained to happen—in the age of grace:

- "Now to Him that is of power to stablish you according to my gospel, and the preaching of Jesus Christ, according to **the revelation of the mystery, which…kept secret since the world began. But is now made manifest**…." **(Romans 16:26.27)**

Biblical Truths:

The gospel of John records where Jesus was instructing Pilate concerning truth. It prompted Pilate to inquire, "What is truth?" Jesus answered that question earlier in prayer to His Father on behalf of His Apostles. He said, "Sanctify them through Thy truth," and added, **"Thy Word is Truth."** On that basis, the Bible represents the primary source of information contained in this book. The Word of God includes details for dealing with every situation in life and essential truths concerning man's purpose, goals, past, present, and future. The Old Testament segment includes the same Holy Scriptures shared by the religion of Judaism. The New Testament is unique only to Christianity. Many consider the Bible the only absolute because it has withstood time and testing throughout history and prophecy.

Almost everything in life requires learning, training, and schooling. You would not attempt to pilot a passenger jet without understanding the instructions and knowledge of the controls. In the same way, it would be unwise to go about life on earth without any directives to follow. Thankfully, that was not the case. God provided clear and firm guidelines so we could enjoy an enriched and purposeful existence. Even so, His intentions demand that you and I read, and heed, understand, and apply those principles to avoid the pitfalls of life. Only by obeying the rules can we overcome the problems and challenges confronting us daily. If you seek answers in the wrong places, you should expect to encounter difficulties.

Romans 3:4 states, "...let God be true, but every man a liar...." We must be realistic about what constitutes accurate answers and seek them from God's perspective and not man's. The Bible is of a validating nature that, with the following passage, provides the assurance it shall always remain the same. Jesus said, **"Heaven and earth shall pass away, but My Words shall not pass away"** (Matthew 24:35). Jesus made this promise over 2000 years ago and try as they have to do away with it; His Word is still with us today.

What about Errors:
A careful study of the Bible is required to absorb its instructions. The Word declares, "Study to show thyself approved unto God...." It would be unfitting for God to fill the Bible full of errors when He told us it is a book to study carefully. Could it be trusted if it contained even one error? Moreover, if someone found one inaccuracy, could not another also exist? Who is to say this, or that is an error—are we the judge of wrongs in the Bible? As a result, we believe the Bible contains and is the source of all truth. We shall find full justification behind those beliefs as we progress in our study.

Secular Confusion:

Sometimes Bible passages appear to the worldly mind as lies or contradictions. Several indicators provide clues as to why this could occur. Some Scriptures may have dual meanings in which one passage discloses two events differently. Sometimes disagreements arise because both transactions happened, but the reader cannot correlate the details to their satisfaction. The Bible describes itself as a holy Book designed for the spiritual-minded. The secular mind is not in tune with spiritual expressions, making what they sometimes read look foolish (1 Corinthians 1:18-25). The result puts the reader at odds with the divine truths of the Bible.

When someone attempts to make what they read from a private interpretation, they will likely encounter difficulty. There is a definite distinction between someone reading Scripture from a secular perspective and another employing a spiritual approach. One applies a personal justification, while the other imparts a disclosure as provided by the Spirit of God.

We may endeavor to use our wisdom, but only God can interpret His Word. The Bible concerns the believer and those who desire to become believers. Only through God's Spirit can we attain genuine revelation, especially those passages involving profound doctrinal truths.

Nevertheless, reading the Bible from a worldly perspective or by any means is advantageous. It helps to keep in mind that all spiritual-minded readers came from a secular background at one time in their life. Therefore, to make the Bible come alive for any reader, it is necessary to enter a spiritual approach.

When individuals receive Christ as Lord and Savior, they also receive the Holy Spirit, who dwells within their hearts. The third Person of the Trinity interprets God's Word within the believer. As (1 Corinthians 2:10) states, **"God hath revealed them (the things in the Bible) unto us by His Spirit: For the Spirit searcheth all things, yea, the deep things of God."** A secular analysis develops misinterpretation, which creates errors, confusion, and unbelief. The following verse addresses this concern:

- "But the natural (secular) man receiveth not the things of the Spirit of God: for they are foolishness unto him: neither can he know *them*, because they are spiritually discerned." **(1 Corinthians 2:14)**

The above passage highlights how receiving the Spirit of God enables the reader to receive revelation concerning God's Word. The natural man has yet to receive the Spirit of God. As a result, doctrinal truths will seem foolish even though he may believe he interprets rightly.

Chapter 2
Purpose and History

The general description that most Christian denominations use to explain the Trinity originated from documentation produced by a 4th Century conference of bishops, known as the Nicene Council. That assembly convened in an attempt to combat heresy and set up doctrinal guidelines. The outcome of those discussions provided a decent explanation of the Trinity; however, it soon became apparent that the doctrine still fell short of having any viable answers. As a result, the Trinity continued to retain its identity as a mystery—a reputation that still haunts the Church to this very day.

Scriptural Understanding:

The Bible itself substantiates why the mystic still exists. Luke's gospel presents a statement from Jesus illustrating that the only way we can know the truths of God is when He discloses them to us. The following verse establishes revelation as the key to understanding who God is; and without such, it is merely man's interpretation:

- "All things are delivered to Me of My Father: and no man knoweth who the Son is, but the Father; and who the Father is, but the Son, and *he* to whom the Son will **reveal** *Him*." **(Luke 10:22)**

A biblical understanding of revelations, mysteries, and secrets will help us gain greater insight into the Trinity. For instance, did God purposely keep some things from us, or does the Bible tell us everything we need to know? Let us see how ***mysteries, revelations, and secrets*** help us better understand these and other issues.

Mysteries:

A mystery is something secret or unknown until someone provides an accurate answer. Therefore, placing the Trinity in this category is a matter of reconsideration in light of the following statement:

- "...there is nothing covered, that shall not be revealed; and hid, that shall not be known." **(Matthew 10:26)** *Similar verses appear in (Mark 4:22) and (Luke 8:17 & 12:2)*

The above verse indicates that if a topic in the Bible seems hidden from our knowledge, its disclosure must occur on some occasion. Paul wrote many times about mysteries kept secret from the ages, but now revealed in his time. Today, if one mystery stands out above all others, it is the Trinity. Notice, Jesus did not specify when it should happen, only that its disclosure would occur at some point in time. Now let us look at the next topic that will help tie things together later on.

Revelations:

The definition of revelation is the solving or uncovering of something once regarded as a mystery. For example, a notable passage in Matthew's gospel finds Jesus asking His disciples, "Whom do men say that I am?" When Peter responded, "You are the Christ, the Son of the living God." Jesus then told Peter that no one had revealed this to him but the Father:

- "Flesh and blood has not **revealed** this to you (Peter), but My Father in heaven...." **(Matthew 16:17)**

Notice that no other individual revealed this to Peter, nor did he know it from within himself, but as this passage declares, the Father revealed it to him. Thus, the substance Jesus uses to build His Church upon is revelation, through the Holy Spirit dwelling within the believer and verified in the following passages:

- "But the Comforter, which is the Holy Ghost, whom the Father will send in My name, He will teach you all thing, and bring all things to your remembrance, whatsoever I have said unto you." **(John 14:26)**
- "But the anointing which ye have received of Him abideth in you, and **ye need not that any man teach you**: but as the same anointing teacheth you of all things, and is truth, and is

no lie, and even as it hath taught you, ye shall abide in Him." **(1 John 2:27)**

Both passages affirm that the Holy Ghost will teach you all things. Thus, the infilling of the Holy Ghost imparts the interpretation within the believer. Next, a passage from Isaiah about secrets will increase our awareness of mysteries and revelations.

Secrets:

While both mystery and secret can be interchangeable, some Scriptures present them differently. For example, God provided the following declaration about secrets in the Book of Isaiah:

- "I have **not** spoken in **secret** from the beginning...." **(Isaiah 48:16)**

This passage is a significant statement that declares God has never spoken to us in secret from the beginning. We must consider the context of this passage from Isaiah's time to perceive its objective. Using the words "from the beginning" indicates Isaiah is looking back to the first three words in the Bible, "In the beginning...." Specifically, God has revealed everything to us through the Scriptures and has kept nothing secret from the beginning of creation. Because the entire Bible is complete in our day and every passage in plain view for our eyes to see, it signifies that nothing is hidden or secret.

Nevertheless, although we might read a particular passage many times, God may withhold the revelation from us until such time we can grasp its deeper meaning. Yet, despite what we have uncovered about secrets thus far, another matter confronts us concerning things that belong only to God. We find this in the following passage:

- "The secret things belong unto the Lord our God, but the things which are revealed belong to us and to our children forever." **(Deuteronomy 29:29)**

The previous passage from (Isaiah 48:16) may sound contradictory compared to (Deuteronomy 29:29), but it is not. While (Isaiah 48:16) states that God has never kept secrets from the beginning, (Deuteronomy 29:29) declares that God did keep some matters secret. The difference in the two passages is (Isaiah 48:16) pertains to things written, and (Deuteronomy 29:29) relates to issues *not* written in the Bible. Those things not recorded in the Bible belong only to the Lord. In contrast, things recorded in the Bible are not secret because we can see them written down and read them with our eyes.

Of all the secret things that belong to God alone, one stands out more than any other. That mystery concerns, by what means did God always exist? The Bible declares that God is from everlasting to everlasting but does not detail how it came about. Undoubtedly, many other happenings have occurred over time eternal that may never even enter our minds, but only God has experienced those encounters.

In other ways, the Bible may provide information concerning an issue yet does not disclose the whole story. One such situation involves a statement Jesus made that "no man, or angel, or even Jesus Himself knows the day or hour of His return to earth, but the Father only." This issue has prompted many to invoke a question, "If Jesus is God, why doesn't He also know when He will return?" We shall address this matter and show why Jesus could not know as we advance in our study. For now, realizing the specifics of mysteries, secrets, and revelations will benefit significantly in later chapters.

Trinity's Central Personality:

When was the last time you had a conversation about the Trinity? Your answer is probably rarely or never like most people, even though this particular topic is perhaps humanity's most important. Why? Because within its boundaries resides the source of your eternal redemption. While on earth, Jesus made some direct statements about the status He holds regarding salvation. In (John 10:30), He presented this proclamation, "I and *My* Father are One," and in (John 14:6) He disclosed that He is the only way to the Father. In another passage (John 8:24), Jesus yielded this warning, "…if ye believe not that I am He, ye shall die in your sins." No individual in history has ever made such bold proclamations and authenticated them with healing and miracles, as did Jesus.

He restored the eyes of the blind, the ears of the deaf, and the tongues of the dumb. He healed the sick, cleansed the lepers, and raised the dead. Yet, all those healings, miracles, and statements disclose a unique meaning regarding salvation. In addition, His death, burial, and resurrection provided a pardon for every sin ever committed. Nevertheless, it also means that each individual must make a decision concerning their life on earth. If we reject Jesus as Lord, we reject the salvation He provided as a payment for our sins (Romans 10:9.10).

Early Church History:

Because the apostles understood who Jesus was and assumed the same in their writings, the Trinity never became an issue to the Church of the 1st Century. The initial expression of the word Trinity occurred around 150AD as a straightforward way to identify the Godhead. After the term emerged as a primary doctrine, a man named *Arius* (256-336AD) sought to cast doubt upon its teaching. His disagreement concerned the divinity of Jesus Christ. He taught that Jesus could not be God because God never had a beginning, nor was He begotten.

Many embraced *Arius's* opposition, which prompted the Church hierarchy to dispel the heresy by establishing doctrinal guidelines. Therefore, the Church authorities assembled a conclave of bishops in 325AD, known as the First Council of *Nicaea*. That committee produced the *Nicene Creed* and reinforced the Church's position proclaiming Jesus as both God and man. Those guiding principles of the 4th Century are the prevailing explanation that shapes the beliefs shared by most Christian denominations today. Other councils formed at later intervals to reinforce the views from Nicaea. Primarily, each succeeding assembly upheld the deity of Jesus and affirmed the Holy Spirit's divinity to be equal to the Father and the Son. Even so, many today still follow *Arius's* opposition to the Trinity.

Since the apostolic days of a united Church, divisions have occurred within Christianity. Most disagreements arose due to Scripture's interpretation or disobedience to governing authorities. Those differences have spawned numerous denominations over the years. Yet, a few refer to themselves as Christian while entirely rejecting the Trinity. These religions generally have their own set of holy books that line up with *non-Christian* values. Since they incorporate Jesus into their framework, they classify themselves under the umbrella of Christianity and advise their members contrary to what mainline churches and the Bible teach. For that reason, traditional denominations consider these other congregations as operating outside the mainstream.

Religions Reject the Trinity:

Apart from Christianity, all world religions reject the Trinity. This rejection focuses mainly on the refusal to recognize the deity of Jesus Christ. To the believing Christian, the Trinity is the essential tenet of the faith. They maintain that if Jesus were not God, Christianity would bear semblance to most other religions, seeking after the philosophies and doctrines of men.

Judaism is the only other religion that shares the same God as Christianity. While they adhere to a belief in God the Father, they also reject Jesus Christ's deity. For the most part, Judaism recognizes the Holy Spirit but without the significance projected by Christendom. Judaism's conflict with the Trinity stems from a passage mentioned earlier (Deuteronomy 6:4), "Hear, O Israel: The LORD our God is one LORD."

The Documents Unchanged:

The Trinity doctrine eventually came under scrutiny from many sources. After a time, it seemed no one could fully comprehend its distinctive structure, and it soon became classified as a mystery. Since the early Church, biblical scholars and Church leaders today know little more regarding the Trinity than they did back then. The absence of comprehensive answers has kept many away from the Christian faith. The question arises, "If confusion exists among Church leaders concerning such a vital doctrine, why should I join them?" As a result, many seeking to satisfy their spiritual appetite and fill the empty void in their heart have explored other options. Even so, there is only one way to fill the emptiness, and that is through the Trinity.

The Search for Jesus:

Men continue to seek answers about Jesus and His origin. The norm is to write books to misinform the uninformed by projecting what *history* records about Him. Their search will continue until they come to grips with the fact that Jesus came to earth with nothing and left with everything. Since the Bible is the only authoritative source for spiritual matters, it encompasses the lone standard for revealing Jesus and the Trinity.

Defining the Trinity:

The Trinity is a distinctive Christian doctrine that declares that God exists in three Persons: **the Father**, **the Son** (Jesus Christ), and the **Holy Ghost** (the Holy Spirit). Surprisingly, only one Bible verse establishes the *three entities* of the Trinity by spelling out each title by name:

- "Go ye therefore, and teach all nations, baptizing them in the name of the **Father**, and of the **Son**, and of the **Holy Ghost**:" **(Matthew 28:19)**

Besides this single verse in (Matthew 28:19), several other passages either expound upon or allude to God's manifestations in different ways. In one instance, John was baptizing **Jesus** (the Son) and the **Holy Ghost** descended upon Him as a dove, and a **voice from heaven** declared, "...Thou art **My** (the Father's) beloved Son; in Thee I am well pleased" (Luke 3:21.22).

In the Old Testament book of Isaiah, another such occurrence took place. You may notice the first part of this verse from an earlier rendering under the heading of secrets. Could it be a mere coincidence that God, who told us He has never spoken in secret from the beginning, places that statement within in the same verse that declares the Trinity in the Old Testament?

- "Come ye near unto Me, hear ye this; I have not spoken in secret from the beginning; from the time that it was, there *am* I: and now the Lord God, and His Spirit, hath sent Me." **(Isaiah. 48:16)**

In this passage, God is speaking in His second Person **(the Son)**. Breaking the verse down will provide better clarity, "Come ye near unto **Me (the Son)**, hear ye this; **I (the Son)** have not spoken in secret from the beginning; from the time that it was, there *am* **I (the Son)**: and now the **Lord God (the Father)**, and **His Spirit (the Holy Spirit)**, hath sent **Me (the Son)**." Checking passages before and after this Scripture verifies God is speaking and not the prophet Isaiah.

A final example of the Trinity located within the same passage takes place at the time when "The Last Supper" had just ended, and Jesus makes the following statement to His disciples:

- "But the **Comforter, which is the Holy Ghost**, whom the **Father** will send in **My** name, He shall teach you all things, and bring all things to your remembrance, whatsoever I have said unto you." **(John 14:26)**

The above verse is another we visited earlier. The passage's context identifies the Comforter as the Holy Ghost and declares that the **Father** will send the **Holy Ghost** in **Jesus**' name. As we progress further in our pursuit of disclosing the mystery, we will meet other passages that illustrate the Godhead in a single verse. The Scriptures we have covered thus far will be adequate for our purposes to this point.

In the following chapters, we shall take a closer look at man's physical and spiritual makeup. You will find that the Trinity pertains not only to God but also to humanity. One reason could be that God made man in His image and likeness.

Chapter 3
The Creation of Man

One vital question that seems to occupy the minds of many is that regarding the matter of existence. What is the meaning of life? Why am I here? No matter what the question, attempting to understand it apart from the Trinity is futile. Awareness is only possible by viewing the Trinity and life as one entity. The Bible states, "For in Him we live and move and have our being…" (Acts 17:28).

The best location to construct an accurate picture of life is where it all began, the book of Genesis. The first chapter finds God creating the heavens and the earth in six days. Yet, through all the handiwork that He established upon the earth, remarkably, the *last* creature He created was a man:

- "And God said, Let Us make man in Our image, after Our likeness: and let them have dominion over the fish of the sea, and over the fowl of the air, and over the cattle, and over all the earth, and over every creeping thing that creepeth upon the earth." **(Genesis 1:26)**

This passage contains the first mention of a man in Scripture, and it speaks volumes concerning his importance in life. He acquired authority over everything else, but most notably, God made man in His image and likeness. Another account of man's creation is recorded in (Genesis 2:7), yet this time, presented with a little more detail. Although the entire content of the verse consists of only 27 words, its significance is invaluable for understanding the Trinity:

- "And the LORD God formed man of the dust of the ground, and breathed into his nostrils the breath of life; and man became a living soul." **(Genesis 2:7)**

The Flesh and the Soul:

The above verse provides a somewhat condensed view of man's composition. Simply put, the dust of the ground became the visible substance. The breath that God breathed into his nostrils formed the invisible life force called a living soul. Several other actions occurred in this verse, which we shall expound upon later.

We can only surmise that Adam was full of life and ready to experience existence as the first human being. His heart began pumping pure, uncontaminated blood throughout his body. His eyes could see; he could hear and do all the things expected of his bodily senses. He could think, have feelings, and do the things anticipated of the mind and soul. Overall, Adam's whole being was operating flawlessly, free of infections, deteriorations, or diseases. It seems that God's original design intended for man to live forever.

As expected, many things took place within those 27 words in (Genesis 2:7). Some things were evident because the verse says so. Others were apparent because we have general knowledge and understanding of how the human body functions. Looking further into Genesis chapter 2 will provide two more passages, which will help us absorb what takes place a little later in Genesis chapter 3.

The Forbidden Tree:
- "And the LORD God commanded the man, saying, Of every tree of the garden thou mayest freely eat: But of the tree of the knowledge of good and evil, thou shalt not eat of it: for in the day that thou eatest thereof thou shalt surely die." **(Genesis 2:16.17)**

God Made Woman:
- "And the LORD God caused a deep sleep to fall upon Adam, and he slept: and He took one of his ribs, and closed up the flesh instead thereof. And the rib, which the LORD God had taken from man, made He a woman, and brought her unto the man." **(Genesis 2:21.22)**

The Creation of Man

At first, God created man in His image and likeness. He instructed the man to multiply, replenish, subdue, and take authority over all the earth. However, (Genesis 2:16.17) discloses one specific commandment given to Adam that reshapes the mood of the circumstances from that point on. The other verse (Genesis 2:21.22) reveals how God made the first woman, who was to be a helpmate for Adam.

Genesis Chapter 3:

Looking at the third chapter, we find a serpent deceiving the woman by enticing her to partake of the forbidden fruit from the tree of the knowledge of good and evil:

- "And the serpent said unto the woman, Ye shall not surely die: For God doth know that in the day that ye eat thereof, then your eyes shall be opened, and ye shall be as gods, knowing good and evil. And when the woman saw that the tree *was* good for food, and that it *was* pleasant to the eyes, and a tree to be desired to make *one* wise, she took of the fruit thereof, and did eat, and gave also unto her husband with her; and he did eat." **(Genesis 3:4-6)**

In light of Adam and Eve eating of the forbidden tree, the remainder of Genesis chapter 3 provides the following details concerning their disobedience and departure from the Garden:

1. The man and woman became aware they were naked, and God knew they had sinned.
2. God alerted the serpent that He would put enmity between the serpent's seed and the seed of the woman.
3. God informed Eve that she would bring forth children in sorrow, and her desire would be to her husband, who would rule over her.
4. God cursed the ground and told Adam he would till it and eat of it all the days of his life until he returned to the dust from whence he came. God then banished Adam and Eve from the Garden.

Because of Adam's sin, the natural part of man began a process whereby it would eventually die and go back to the dust of the ground from where it originated. Thus, God established the Scripture "... for dust thou art, and unto dust thou shalt return" (Genesis 3:19).

Obedience to a Serpent:

The reality of sin today is a result of what happened in the Garden. It only took a few choice words from a serpent to change the entire situation. Who was the serpent that deceived Eve? The passage in (Genesis 3:14) hints he was part of the cattle species and cursed above all the beast of the field for enticing the woman. The Bible calls him Satan in (Revelation 12:9). He must have been an upright creature capable of talking because God did not curse the beast to crawl on its belly until after the disobedience occurred. Some believe the serpent may have been as close to human as any beast in the creation. Others consider he could be the clue to the so-called missing link science has long sought after. Most scholars agree that Satan inhibited and talked through the serpent. This interpretation would be consistent with instances where Jesus cast out demonic spirits who spoke through the individuals they possessed.

Comparing Scripture with Scripture:
- "For all that is in the world, the lust of the flesh, the lust of the eyes, and the pride of life, is not of the Father, but is of the world." **(1 John 2:16)**

The above New Testament passage provides an interesting contrast when compared with (Genesis 3:4-6). What happened at *the fall of man* corresponds with (1 John 2:16) above in that Eve saw that the tree was good for food (the lust of the flesh), was pleasant to the eyes (the lust of the eyes), and desired to make one wise (the pride of life). The Bible speaks of Satan as the god of this world and comparing the two passages side-by-side bears witness to that fact.

What happened at *the fall of man* looks as though the woman sinned. However, although she shared a portion of Adam's physical make-up, she did not fully partake in the original creation. God had yet to make Eve in the form of a woman when He gave Adam the commandment. Therefore, Adam shouldered sole responsibility for keeping the commandment as verified in the following passage:
- "Wherefore, as by one man (Adam) sin entered into the world, and death by sin; and so death passed upon all men, for that all have sinned." **(Romans 5:12)**

The Result of Sin:
1.) Separation from God.
2.) Specific curses applied upon humanity, including death.
3.) All humanity inherited a sin-nature.
4.) Sin required finding an acceptable pathway back to God.

The visible part of the man did not die immediately. We find Adam and Eve had sons and daughters, and Adam did not die until 930 years of age. Although God banished them from the Garden, He still permitted them to replenish the earth. If Adam and Eve had died immediately after the fall, there would be no procreation, and as a result, no more humanity. However, God did not want the Creation and His carefully designed objective merely to fall by the wayside. Therefore, He allowed man time to produce children, so the plan He proposed from the beginning would develop as He established it to happen:

- "Having made known unto us the mystery of His will, according to His good pleasure which He hath purposed in Himself:" **(Ephesians 1:9)**

Although they did not die physically until many years later, an examination from a different perspective reveals that they did die immediately—spiritually. The moment they disobeyed God's command, they knew they were naked and thereby acquired the knowledge of good and evil. The spiritual death resulted in separation from God's Spirit (the Source of all life).

Does this mean that God condemned Adam and Eve forever? Not if we consider that "Enoch (the seventh in Adam's lineage) walked with God; and he was not; for God took him." Yes, Adam and Eve sinned, but it was necessary to introduce sin into the world in God's overall plan of salvation.

After their eviction from the Garden, Adam and Eve had only the curse upon them due to their disobedience. The next commandment that God pronounced did not occur until Moses:

- "For until the law sin was in the world; but sin is not imputed when there is no law. Nevertheless death reigned from Adam to Moses, even over them that had not sinned after the similitude of Adam's transgression, who is the figure of Him that was to come." **(Romans 5:13.14)**

Although the charge for sin did not occur until the Mosaic Law came into effect, the sin-nature and death had already passed on through Adam's transgression. When God drove out Adam and Eve from the *Garden*, the tree of knowledge's commandment also banished. God did not impart any new commandments until Moses except for directives to be fruitful, multiply, and abstain from eating blood. Without a law given, there would be no sin. Even those destroyed in the flood received a chance to repent (1 Peter 4:19.20). If God never bestowed the one commandment upon Adam, he would have lived forever and his offspring likewise. However, that would have produced a problem for God.

The Remedy:

It was essential for man to have a free will to love God in return. That was the only way it could happen. Without a free will, he would be as a robot, unable to make his own decisions and *forced* to love God and obey His commandments. By employing his free will, man can choose to accept God's love and fellowship or reject them. That means God cannot decide for us to love Him; the choice remains solely in our hands.

Many pose the question, "Why didn't God simply save everyone and Jesus would not have to die?" It seems like a simple enough solution, but maybe not. We do *not* know when God initiated the idea to create man—"the secret things belong unto the Lord our God." However, we can only surmise that Trinity's purpose was for God to fellowship with someone like unto Himself. Although God had the angels, one-third of them rebelled against Him and followed Satan. Therefore, they also had the privilege of free will since they followed the evil one to his demise. As occurred with the angels who rebelled, so too is it with man, not only today but also throughout history. Many individuals dislike God (the One who created them) to the point of wiping any mention of Him from society. Yet, God still loves man. He paid the price for everyone so He could call them His children. So why doesn't God allow everyone to go to heaven and be with Him forever? Take into account the following scenario:

****

A wealthy individual who owned a large mansion invited enough people to fill his estate and stay in it with him for a whole year—no questions asked. Yet, since he called upon anyone and everyone, little did he know that most of those who took him up on his offer hated him. They would sneer, mock, and curse at him every time they encountered him in his house. This same issue confronted God by allowing humanity to live with Him, not for a year, but eternity. It also explains why God gave man a free will, so he could choose to love Him back. When the angels rebelled, they were in heaven with Him. He did not want that to happen with man. In this manner, He devised the plan of salvation to make sure that those He would call His children were the ones who would love Him in return.

****

Chapter 4
Examining Spiritual Issues

One concern regarding the Trinity deals with our ability to see our bodily features and our inability to observe our spiritual attributes. Consequently, because only the body is perceptible, some even deny the soul and spirit's existence.

Being able to see the physical makes it more of a priority to keep in good shape. For instance, we always feed our bodies but may seldom or never provide for the spiritual. Jesus said, "Man does not live by bread alone, but by every word that proceedeth from the mouth of God." This passage indicates that the spiritual element is also capable of starving for lack of food. If we could see our soul, we would probably spend more time attending to its needs. In essence, we identify more physically due to our ability to peer into, probe at, and dissect the anatomy's various parts.

One thing the early Church fathers lacked in understanding the Trinity was access to today's technology. Without a doubt, it would render those early saints speechless to see the technological advances, which have occurred in just the past century. Of the many modern innovations made available through technology, none warrants more merit for our purposes than those found within the health sector. Research in this specific field provides insight into genetics, anatomy, blood, DNA, and other related practices. One central area of importance concerns the reproductive development of an infant within its mother's womb.

Yet, while studies in these various health fields can look at tiny details and generate a highly structured physical profile, we also need to find a way to gaze into the spiritual. The foremost concern in dealing with spiritual issues is that it remains a gray area seemingly impossible to explore with our natural senses. Still, it is essential to understand the various elements of man in order to realize the Trinity. Keep in mind; God made man in His image and likeness. The Bible declares, "God is a Spirit," yet man has a body, soul, and spirit. So what are the necessary steps to track down information about the spiritual make-up of man?

While health studies involve the human side, their findings do not deter the Bible's teachings. By coupling Bible passages with current health advances such as ultrasound and other analytical instruments, we can probe inside the human structure as was never before possible. Although the Bible does not explore microscopic details concerning the unseen, it does provides enough information to harvest a significant picture of man's composition. Depending on how these features interact with one another determines an individual's fallen state or redeemed virtue. The Scriptures we shall look at in this chapter will supply helpful insights into man's makeup and how his body, soul, and spirit work together to make one total individual.

It is worth noting that the (Genesis 2:7) account of the creation of Adam did not cover all the details that occurred within that one verse. We know this because the Bible lists additional information in other Scripture passages. One of those particulars reveals that the Spirit of God also entered through Adam's nostrils along with the breath of life. For a better insight into this, let us look at three distinct passages from the book of Job. God rebukes three of Job's four closest friends for speaking wrongly against him at the end of that particular book. The fourth man, named Elihu, God did not accuse. The following three passages find Job speaking in the first verse, and Elihu finishes with the final two:

- "As God liveth, who hath taken away my judgment; and the Almighty, who hath vexed my soul; all the while my **breath** is in me, and the **Spirit of God** is in my nostrils; my lips shall not speak wickedness, nor my tongue utter deceit." **(Job 27:2-4)**
- "The **Spirit of God** hath made me, and the **breath** of the Almighty hath given me life." **(Job 33:4)**

- "If He set His heart upon man, *if* He gather unto Himself **His Spirit** and **His breath**; all flesh shall perish together, and man shall turn again unto dust." **(Job 34:14.15)**

Notice, all three passages make mention of breath and the Spirit of God. Two verses reveal that the Spirit of God resides within man. This detail is noteworthy because it indicates that God's Spirit dwells within the believer and the non-believer. It could also explain what Jesus meant when He told the Pharisees, "the Kingdom of God is within them" (Luke 17:21). Jesus did not say they possessed the Kingdom of God but that the ability to access it resided within them—through the Spirit of God.

The first passage above (Job 27:2-4) indicates God's Spirit did not reside within the heart but the nostril area. Again, this would be consistent with what Jesus told the Pharisees, "The Kingdom of God was within them," howbeit only within the nostril area. Since the crucifixion had not yet occurred, the Holy Spirit was unavailable for salvation. That event happened on the feast of Pentecost, ten days after Christ's ascension into heaven. When redemption occurs, the Holy Spirit resides within the heart of the believer.

The next verse above (Job 33:4) restates the importance of God's Spirit and His breath. The final verse (Job 34:14.15) reveals that all flesh would perish if God ever took back His Spirit and breath from humanity.

In the Genesis account, we found that God *first* formed Adam from the dust of the ground. Then God breathed the breath of life into his nostrils. Lastly, God made Adam a living soul. These events' timelines *should* follow natural birth, even though the reproductive cycle takes much longer. In the final analysis, we find we are dealing with *five* main issues of concern: the breath of life, the body, the soul, the spirit of man, and the Spirit of God.

The Physical and Spiritual Nature of Man:

Did anything physically exist before the Creation? The Bible does not expound upon this issue to any degree. However, when it came time for God to make man, the necessary material already existed—dust. Thus, man became a by-product of an earthly substance:

- "And the Lord God formed man of the dust of the ground, and breathed into his nostrils the breath of life; and man became a living soul." **(Genesis 2:7)**

The above verse only mentions three things:
1. The Lord God formed man of the dust of the ground.
2. God breathed into his nostrils the breath of life.
3. The man became a living soul.

The first thing to notice of the happenings mentioned above is that the transformation of dust to flesh occurred before Adam became a living soul. The next incident finds the breath of life entering into the nostrils while the form is still dust. Somewhere in this interim is where (Genesis 2:7) does not inform us. However, (Job) and other Scriptures disclose that the Spirit of God lives within man. Therefore, the Spirit of God needed to enter into Adam's nostrils along with the breath of life. In addition, at that same time frame, God formed Adam's spirit within him according to (Zechariah 12:1). That brings us to the third event whereby Adam became a living soul.

For a more detailed look, the Spirit of God and the spirit of Adam had to enter into the nostrils at the same time as did the breath of life. The reasoning is, when salvation occurs, the Spirit of God joins with man's spirit (located within the heart of his being) and thereby radiates life into his soul. Thus, Adam was a living soul, as the (Genesis 2:7) passage states. However, when Adam sinned, separation of God's Spirit from man's spirit took place, meaning his soul no longer received life. As (Job 27:2-4) alleges, the Spirit of God did not depart completely but remained in the nostril area instead of the heart.

The Physical Aspects of Man:
Although there is a lack of information regarding the various cells, organs, and other essentials that made up Adam's body, we know the verse naturally integrates them within. Another detail worth mentioning; we found an additional passage bearing what happened after the breath of life entered Adam's nostrils. This verse states, "…the life of the flesh is in the blood" (Leviticus 17:11). Consequently, once the dust transformed into the lifeless

body, cells and other elements were present within—including the heart. However, blood did not begin flowing through the heart and other bodily components until after the breath of life penetrated the nostrils. Because blood requires oxygen, the breath of life supplied respiration to the lungs and permitted blood to flow throughout the system.

Five Things That Took Place at the Creation of Man:
   1). The dust transformed into the physical man.
   2). The breath of life supplied oxygen for the blood.
   3). God formed a spirit within Adam (Zechariah 12:1).
   4). God placed His Spirit within the man.
   5). God made man a living soul.

Adam's Rib and Eve's Formation:

Genesis 2:21.22 records the forming of the woman from Adam's rib, yet (Genesis 5:2) places Eve in the original Creation. However, although she was already present in his rib, she was not present with Adam when God gave him the commandment to abstain from the forbidden fruit. As God took from the earth to create the male, He used a bone from the man to produce the woman. That is all we know in the Bible about how God formed the female. Now let us look at childbirth's physical and spiritual development and compare it to Adam's creation.

The Natural and the Created Progression:

This segment will contrast the natural childbirth's progression to the five issues in Adam's creation. Understanding these details now will help later realizing how Jesus became a Human Being. The cycle begins at conception in natural birth when the male element fertilizes the female's ovum (egg). Without fertilization, the ovum is without life, but once the male component inseminates the egg, it begins the process of a living being. We can equate the sperm during the fertilization process to the breath of life in Adam's creation. Thus, the oxygen for the blood, the Spirit of God, man's spirit, and soul are all contained or formed within the male seed at conception. Conversely, we can consider the ovum as the dust of the ground as it involves the embryo's fleshly state. (Compare to "The Five Issues" cited previously).

For the most part, the spiritual is of the father, although many physical characteristics of the child's make-up also pass from the male. Meanwhile, the mother supplies the infant's physical necessities while it is in the womb. Gene inheriting factors provided by the mother carries on with the infant after its birth.

Following fertilization, life and the presence of blood become evident within the embryo. Throughout the stages of pregnancy, the infant takes on human qualities, and around four months, an ultrasound will detect a heartbeat and an image of the fetus. In contrast to Adam's creation, both parents share the gene inheriting characteristics integrated into the infant's natural birth.

Job's passages have established that everyone has the Spirit of God living within them, if only in the nostril area. As with Adam at his creation, the Spirit of God is present and united with the infant's spirit. Meanwhile, oxygen for the embryo flows through the fluid-filled placenta. Medical health science provides evidence that not one drop of the mother's blood mingles with the baby's blood while it is within the mother's womb. The male seed introduces the only blood encountered for the infant. That means that even though the heart pumps blood throughout the infant's body, it originated from the male element at fertilization.

Natural birth establishes the infant's spirit, God's Spirit, and even the gender of the child at insemination. During pregnancy and at delivery, the baby is in a state of grace. When the child is young, it still has life from the Spirit of God living within the heart. As long as the young person has not sinned, he or she remains a child of God. However, when this individual reaches the age of accountability (whatever age it is) and transgression occurs, the Spirit of God departs from the child's spirit. Some referred to this as spiritual death. Thus, the soul is void of life, and therefore, must become born-again by the Spirit of God. The apostle Paul illustrates this in (Romans 7:9), "For I was alive without the law once; but **when the commandment came,** sin revived (or came around), and I died." This same scenario played out in Adam's situation. He was alive without the law once; that is before God gave him the decree not to eat from the forbidden tree. Therefore, when the commandment came, and sin occurred, he died.

Jesus once remarked, "Suffer not the little children to come to Me, for such are the Kingdom of Heaven." In another place, He added, "Unless you become as a little child you cannot enter into the Kingdom of Heaven." The conclusion is that the child is free from sin until the age of accountability.

Observation:

The discovery of this chapter recognizes that salvation is not of the physical but of the spiritual. Even so, it is still beyond the genius of even the most advanced technology to probe into issues of a spiritual nature. Connecting some of the latest highly developed technological expertise with Scripture passages has helped open many previous unknowns. Yet, even without ultrasound, the reality that a baby is alive within the womb of its mother is evident by merely observing it moving and witnessing it kicking. Besides, health/science has advanced to understanding even the smallest detail of the birthing cycle from conception to the actual birth.

The main reason for the Trinity is to redeem humanity from certain doom. Ezekiel's 18th chapter clearly explains how each individual is accountable for their sins. We all receive the nature to sin, but our choice determines if we remain in that condition. Ezekiel makes it apparent: "the soul that sinneth, it shall die." Thankfully, the New Testament's age of grace offers a simplified method of salvation through repentance by confessing and believing by faith:

- "That if thou shalt confess with thy mouth the Lord Jesus, and shalt believe in thine heart that God hath raised Him from the dead, thou shalt be saved." **(Romans 10:9)**

Chapter 5
The Totality of Man

The previous chapter mentioned that the body, soul, and spirit made up the total man. Since man is also a triune being, it may prove helpful to take an even closer look at the totality of man. Much like we found with the Trinity where only one Bible verse mentioned the Father, Son, and Holy Ghost, we also see the body, soul, and spirit referenced together in only one verse. Here we find Paul encouraging the brethren at Thessalonica:

- "… and *I pray God* your whole **spirit and soul and body** be preserved blameless unto the coming of our Lord Jesus Christ." **(1 Thessalonians 5:23)**

Other Old or New Testament passages link the body, soul, and spirit together without mentioning the three by name in the same verse. An example listed in (Hebrews 4:12) presents the soul and spirit but illustrates the body by a different set of features; namely the joints and marrow:

- "For the Word of God *is* quick, and powerful, and sharper than any two-edged sword, piercing even to the dividing asunder of **soul and spirit, and of the joints and marrow**, and *is* a discerner of the thoughts and intents of the heart." **(Hebrews 4:12)**

Understanding the purposes and characteristics of the body, soul, and spirit will shed light on how closely they relate to each other in unison with God's image and likeness. Therefore, this chapter will use Scripture passages to illustrate how individuals interact to embody one total being.

1) The Body:

It is necessary to focus on Adam and sin to sort out the variables connecting man's components to the Trinity. The characteristics of the body are familiar to most of us. Although many internal and external parts make up the body's structure, the composite still adds to one individual. Nevertheless, the only part of the physical attributes we need to consider within the scope of the Trinity is the heart.

1a.) The Heart:

The core feature of the body is the heart. This vital instrument sends life-giving blood to the cells and organs. When the heart stops, the physical body dies and eventually returns to the dust. Simultaneously, the soul begins a separate venture to the place the individual chose in his lifetime as the place he would spend his eternal afterlife. We can *also* define the word heart in a spiritual sense as the dwelling place that the ***spirit*** fills (i.e., *the heart of a man*).

2.) The Soul:

The soul is the immortal focal point in man that encases his desires, emotions, and will. It is the part made in God's image and likeness and lives on after physical death. Because of sin, the soul decides which of the other two entities it desires to follow. The soul has the choice to pursue the influences of the flesh or the things of the spirit. A dead soul searches for something to fill the void created within the heart by sin. The following passages provide further particulars concerning the soul.

2a.) What Happens to the Soul at Death?

A passage from (1 Kings 17) clarifies that the soul *departs* from the physical body after death. Here we find Elijah praying for a dead child's soul to return to him:

- "And he stretched himself upon the child three times, and cried unto the Lord, and said, O Lord my God, I pray Thee, let this child's soul come into him again. And the Lord heard the voice of Elijah; and **the soul** of the child came into him again, and he revived." **(1 Kings 17:21.22)**

2b.) Love God With all thy Soul:

The following passage illustrates the first of all commandments.

It expresses the relationship of the soul as the center of desires, emotions, and will. Also, notice that the mind is separate from the soul. The same context three verses later (Mark 12:33) expresses the mind as the understanding, while the Greek translates the same word (**mind**) in this setting, as the thoughts and imaginations.

- "And thou shalt love the Lord thy God with all thy heart, and with all **thy soul**, and with all thy mind, and with all thy strength: this is the first commandment." **(Mark 12:30)**

2c.) Independence of the Soul and Spirit:

This following Scripture displays both the soul and the spirit in the same verse and distinguishes how the two react. Mary's soul expresses real emotions as she magnifies the Lord. However, Mary's spirit demonstrates a spiritual application by worshiping her Savior. Thus, we find the passage portrays the soul and spirit as distinctly separate entities:

- "And Mary said, **My soul** doth magnify the Lord, and my spirit hath rejoiced in God my Saviour." **(Luke 1:46.47)**

2d.) Separation of the Soul and Spirit:

We saw this passage earlier in this chapter. It shows the closeness of the soul and spirit as the two entities dwell within the body. Although we cannot see the soul and spirit, to put them into perspective, the proximity of the joints and marrow is as close as it gets. This unification also puts a salvation perspective on the intimacy of the Spirit of God and the living soul:

- "For the Word of God *is* quick, and powerful, and sharper than any two-edged sword, piercing even to the dividing asunder of **soul and spirit, and of the joints and marrow**, and *is* a discerner of the thoughts and intents of the heart." **(Hebrews 4:12)**

2e.) Consequence:

This final verse shows the importance and worth of the soul. In a question, "Is the soul worth exchanging for a billion-dollar lottery ticket, all the gold in the world, all the cars on the road, all the houses, lands, and diamonds, and cruise ships? What about everything mentioned together?" However, many individuals are selling their very soul for nothing in exchange, but eternal destruction:

- "For what shall it profit a man if he shall gain the whole world, and lose his own soul? Or what shall a man give in exchange for **his soul**?" **(Mark 8:36.37)**

3.) The Spirit:
Ruach is the Hebrew word for spirit, and Pneuma is Greek. Both meanings signify to blow, breathe, or spirit. We can define the spirit of man as the controlling influence and focal point of his affections. Often referred to as the life principle God infused into man and the part that desires to worship and serve Him. The body, soul, and spirit initially relate to one another in the following manner: the body receives life from the blood; the soul gets its life from the spirit of man, which receives its life from the Spirit of God. The following Scriptures provide references to man's spirit.

3a.) What Happens to the Spirit at Death?
This particular passage provides a view of the separate directions the body and the spirit take at the time of death:
- "Then shall the dust return to the earth as it was: and **the spirit** shall return unto God who gave it." **(Ecclesiastes 12:7)**

3b.) The Location of our spirit:
This verse discloses where the spirit dwells within an individual:
- "I Daniel was grieved in my **spirit** in the **midst** of *my* body." **(Daniel 7:15)**

3c.) How the Lord Searches the Soul:
Next, we find God using man's spirit like a candle to search the belly's inward parts. A previous passage disclosed the closeness of the soul and spirit, which this passage undoubtedly portrays:
- "**The spirit** of man *is* the candle of the LORD, searching all the inward parts of the belly (soul)." **(Proverbs 20:27)**

3d.) How God Knows you as His Child:
In the next verse, we find the Holy Spirit bearing witness to the born-again spirit. Life from God is radiating life into man's spirit as the heart of God unites with the heart of man:
- "The Spirit itself beareth witness with our **spirit**, that we are the children of God:" **(Romans 8:16)**

3e.) Origin of our Spirit:

This final passage verifies that God formed a spirit in man. The fact is, when God breathed into man's nostrils, there was no disclosure of man even having a spirit. The first mention did not occur until the 41st chapter of Genesis. The following verse from the Book of Zechariah verifies that God formed a spirit within man:

- "The burden of the word of the LORD for Israel, saith the LORD, which stretcheth forth the heavens, and layeth the foundation of the earth, and **formeth the spirit of man within him**." **(Zechariah 12:1)**

The Spiritual Application:

The previous assortment of Scriptures provided a look into man's body, soul, and spirit regarding the total man. Now let us break down the totality into more descriptive terms:

- The **body** (flesh or outer man) is the physical entity that houses the soul and spirit. It accommodates the five senses, contains the blood, performs necessary work, and represents personal recognition. Regarding salvation, the flesh is the component that the unregenerate soul seeks after.

- The **soul** (inner man) is the life force within man and is the nucleus of his desires, will, and emotions. The soul operates as the controlling force of the flesh and is the eternal part of man. The dwelling place for the soul is within the body while the individual remains alive on earth. It embodies the spiritual component made in the image of God. Thus, the soul is the deciding factor regarding eternal salvation.

- The **spirit** (heart) is the life source and the conduit through which the Spirit of God flows. It also serves as the focal point of the individual's affections toward God.

One Final Look—This Time in Reverse:

To gain additional insight, let us take one more glance at the progression of the total man, but this time in reverse order:

- **"The Spirit of God"** (the Life Source): Sin separated us from God, but His Spirit did not entirely leave. It still resides within the head or nostrils part of man. While God's Spirit supplies

Life to man's spirit, sin blocks and prevents it from happening. When an individual exercises the free will to call upon the name of Jesus, only then can he break free from his sin and allow the Spirit of God to flow and reunite with his spirit.

- **"The spirit of man"** (the heart of man) is the conduit for God's Spirit to flow through, thereby providing Life for the soul. However, unless the individual calls upon Jesus for eternal life, the Spirit of God cannot flow into his spirit.

- **"The soul"** (the dominant force): made in God's image. The soul decides from which entity it desires to receive life. It chooses between mortal life from the flesh and eternal life through the spirit.

- **"The body"** (the flesh): When the soul (initially alive) finds itself as a dead soul, it instinctively seeks after life. Sin shuts off the Life flow of God's Spirit and prevents it from penetrating man's spirit. Realizing that Life comes from his spirit man and finding it void, he seeks life from any source and finds it in his flesh.

The natural (unsaved) man receives his life from the flesh and seeks after the world to gratify his spiritual hunger. Sensing something missing, he attempts to justify existence through religion or by endeavoring to be righteous or the impossible task of keeping the commandments. However, none of these things erases sin. Only when an individual realizes that Jesus already paid the price for his offenses and calls upon His name for salvation can the Father send Life-saving grace from the Holy Spirit into the man's heart. Coming up, we shall see what role blood has to play in the overall picture.

Chapter 6
The Blood

The last chapter illustrated the body as performing the physical tasks while the soul and spirit carried out the spiritual responsibilities. We did not find three men performing different chores, but one man utilizing three distinct attributes to achieve one common purpose.

Similarly, *God's* three individualities also perform different tasks while they derive from the same origin. Each separate entity shares a mutual relationship within. For instance, God is the Source of Life. While that designation applies to the Father, it is also applicable to the Son and Holy Ghost. Throughout the Bible, we find valuable insights into the structure and characteristics of God. This next feature, however, is one of exceptional interest regarding the Trinity.

Two Expressions of the Blood:

The Book of Genesis records God resuming His salvation plan nearly two thousand years after creating Adam. In doing so, He selected a man named Abraham through whom He would make a covenant:

"And I will give unto thee, and to thy seed after thee, the land wherein thou art a stranger, all the land of Canaan, for an everlasting possession; and I will be their God." **(Genesis 17:8)**

"And you shall circumcise the flesh of your foreskin; and it shall be a token of the covenant betwixt Me and you." **(Genesis 17:11)**

The promise of God and the circumcision of every male seed of Abraham guaranteed the covenant's legality. This pledge was, in effect, a blood covenant for the Jewish people. However, some 2000 years later, God made another covenant, this time using His own blood. At the "Last Supper," Jesus lifted up the cup, gave it to His apostles, and said:

- "…drink ye all of it: for this is **the blood of the new testament**, which is shed for many for the remission of sins." **(Matthew 26:28)**

We generally think of blood in the physical realm, as we see it with our natural sight. When Adam sinned, his blood changed from pure to a corrupted substance. The result caused his body to deteriorate to the point of ultimate physical death. However, when referring to the blood of Jesus, we must look at it differently. Even though His blood still consists of a natural physical substance, it is not earthy or contaminated by sin. A passage from the first epistle of John depicts the blood of Jesus spiritually to man. It shows that the blood He shed on Calvary's cross washes away all the sins we have generated within our lives:

- "…**the blood** of Jesus Christ His Son cleanseth us from **all** sin." **(1 John 1:7)**

From a biblical viewpoint, what concerns us here is that blood originates from both a physical and a spiritual perspective. Each view came into play when Cain killed his brother Able (Genesis 4:10). The blood was visible on the ground and invisible as it cried out to God. As a result, the physical and spiritual narratives occurred during the same event.

Blood also plays a dual role concerning man. Its relevance factors in when we see what purpose the blood plays in both the sin-nature and the atonement for sins. The following passage also displays the same two characteristics of the blood:

- "For the **life of the flesh** is in the blood: and I have given it to you upon the altar to make an atonement for your souls: for it is the blood *that* maketh an **atonement for the soul.**" **(Leviticus 17:11)**

This passage displays the visible blood as the life of the flesh, and it performs a different role by becoming atonement for the soul. Everyone's blood is of a physical substance within a spiritual domain. While the blood of Jesus also exhibited the same distinct attributes ascribed to humanity, it stems from a different situation. The purpose of His blood was to make atonement for the soul. Yet, since our eyes cannot peer into the sphere of the unseen, the only way to make contact with it is by faith.

The Fact of Faith:

The Bible defines faith as "… the substance of things hoped for, the evidence of things not seen" (Hebrews 11:1). We cannot see the blood covering Christ shed, but we must believe it exists to receive it. That applies to everything regarding the affairs within the spirit world. Jesus said, "When you pray, believe that you receive and you shall have." Although we cannot see our prayers, we must believe they go up and that God hears and will answer them.

From the (Hebrew 11:1) definition given above, when we make Jesus our Lord, it activates a measure of our faith. Consequently, the Spirit of God produces a restoration of new life for the soul. This action results in an awareness of a changed nature that transforms faith into fact. When the Spirit lives inside, salvation is satisfied and verified by the faith of the reality within.

The Sin-Nature:

The same characteristics (physical and spiritual) detected in the blood are also established within the fabric of sin. The following example originates from a statement Jesus made. It concerns first physically looking at and then spiritually lusting in the heart:

- "Ye have heard that it was said by them of old time, Thou shalt not commit adultery: But I say unto you, That whosoever looketh on a woman to lust after her hath committed adultery with her already **in his heart." (Matthew 5:27.28)**

Notice that the lust of the eyes initiated the adultery physically, and the desires of the flesh formed it, not physically, but spiritually within his heart. Thus, the following passage is a prelude to how Adam's sin caused death and created a sin-nature in humanity:

- "Wherefore, as by one man (Adam) sin entered into the world, and death by sin; and so death passed upon all men, for that all have sinned." **(Romans 5:12)**

The question is, how does Adam's sin pass on to all men? To answer this, we might consider a different passage from Romans:
- "Concerning His Son Jesus Christ our Lord, which was made of the seed of David **according to the flesh**." **(Romans 1:3)**

The term "made according to the flesh" might seem as though Jesus' lineage would revert to Adam, whereby He acquired sin. Yet, other passages proclaim that Jesus had no sin. Therefore, sin could not pass through the **flesh**, or else it would have infected Jesus. Also, it cannot occur through the **spirit** because the spirit does not contain sin. The book of (Ecclesiastes 12:7) records that the **spirit** goes back to God who gave it, and sin cannot enter into heaven. Neither could the **soul** be the sin-nature's path because each person has a soul that does not forward to others. That leaves only one viable means for the sin-nature to take place. Since sin corrupted Adam's **blood**, and because the male supplies the entire amount of the infant's blood, it substantiates that blood is the channel through which the sin-nature passes.

An earlier chapter reveals that the mother supplies the infant's physical attributes, while the father provides the spiritual, including the blood. Thus, the sin-nature spiritually passes on to all men through the physical blood of Adam. Yet, it did not pass on to Jesus because His *bloodline* did not revert to Adam but God.

The Blood Connection:

The infected blood of Adam passes on to everyone in a physical fashion. It happens in the conception process through the fertilization of the ovum. Each subsequent male acquires the ability to pass on the tainted blood to his offspring. However, embedded within the contaminated blood is the sin-nature. It is of a spiritual makeup, which yields a desire to sin.

When Adam sinned, his infected blood caused his flesh to deteriorate until, at some point, he would die. Thus, Adam's blood became the means to introduce sin-nature into the world. It also meant that every offspring of Adam would die both physically and spiritually.

When we view the various genealogies in the Bible, the bloodline follows through the male's ancestry. This reality holds for anyone searching for their family tree. In each case, it reverts through a list of male recipients, eventually winding up at Adam.

Because each male supplies all the blood to his offspring, they too receive the sin-nature. Such was the case with Adam. His blood, including the sin-nature embedded therein, forwarded on to each of his future descendants:

- "(God has) made of **one blood** all nations of men to dwell on all the face of the earth, and hath determined the times before appointed, and the bounds of their habitation;" **(Acts 17:26)**

God's Spiritual Application:

Adam's sin also caused a separation between God's Spirit and Adam's spirit, and from that point on, the corrupted blood continued to pass to the next generation without a way to stop the process. Because no one was capable of having their blood purified to the point of making it incorruptible, humanity was doomed. However, blood also has another application, and that is for atonement. Therefore, through God's infinite wisdom, He devised a plan to use a type of "blood sacrifice" to atone for the sins of man:

- "...and I have given **it** to you upon the altar to make an atonement for your souls: for it *is* the blood *that* maketh an atonement for the soul." **(Leviticus 17:11)**

God provided a way to use blood as a channel to draw man back to Himself. This action offered a substitute absolution for sin. Looking at the blood from the Old Testament's basis for atonement, the sacrificial rituals of bulls and goats did not take away sin or remove the sin-nature but covered them for a season. The high priest went into the tabernacle to sprinkle animal blood on the altar. Although it was essential that animals selected for the sacrifices be without spot or blemish, the blood was not a perfect sacrifice because the high priest performed this ceremony every year. A passage from Habakkuk discloses something significant concerning God, "Thou art of purer eyes than to behold evil, and canst not look on iniquity..." (Habakkuk 1:13). God cannot look on iniquity, but if covered by the blood sacrifice to atone for sin, He can look upon it but notices only the blood:

- "Forasmuch as ye know that ye were not redeemed with corruptible things, as silver and gold..., but with the precious blood of Christ, as of a lamb without blemish and without spot." **(1 Peter 1:18.19)**

The Old Testament atonement was merely a shadow of the blood, which Jesus shed once for all time. He became the ultimate sinless sacrifice offered once for all men. His blood was without spot or blemish as required by God for the atonement. He also became the High Priest designated to perform those duties:

- "...we have a great **High Priest**, that is passed into the heavens, Jesus the Son of God...." **(Hebrews 4:14)**

The pure blood that Jesus shed upon the cross at Calvary became the basis for the atonement of every sin committed by every soul. However, only by grace through faith is the atonement applied to cover sin. The following is a picture of the corrupted blood of man changed by the pure blood of Jesus:

- "Come now, and let us reason together, saith the Lord: though your sins be as scarlet, they shall be as white as snow; though they be red like crimson, they shall be as wool." **(Isaiah 1:18)**

Regardless of saved or not, the reality of all individuals is that the physical body shall continue to deteriorate until some point in time it dies. Yet, the unsaved soul remains spiritually dead and forever bound to the choice he made while alive on earth. In contrast, everything is different in this respect for the saved individual. The incorruptible blood of Jesus redeems and cleanses him from all unrighteousness. Although the sin-nature did not disappear from the blood, the desire to sin no longer exists (1 John 3:9). Yet, for the atonement to cover sins, **the reunification of man and God's Spirit must occur to replace spiritual death with eternal life**.

- "Whosoever is born of God doth not commit sin; for His seed remaineth in him: and he cannot sin, for he is born of God." **(1 John 3:9)**
- "...Unto Him (Jesus Christ) that loved us and washed us from our sins in His own **blood**." **(Revelation 1:5)**

****

Made in God's Image:

We looked at the body, soul, and spirit of man in the previous chapter. This may be an excellent place to gather a little more insight into the similarities between God and man. In doing so, it would be worthwhile to look at a passage we came across earlier (Genesis 1:26). Here we find God saying:

- "...let Us make man in Our image, after Our likeness...." **(Genesis 1:26)**

Interestingly, this part of the verse suggests that God is talking to someone. Using the words Us and Our indicates He was talking to Himself since there is only one God. A look at (Genesis 1:2) finds the Spirit of God moving upon the face of the waters, and verse three states, "let there be light." Could it be that God was talking to his own Spirit? Was there a third entity involved? That actuality seems like the only conclusion we can reach. If He were talking to angels, He would not have used the words "Let **Us** make man...." Only God created the original Creation (Genesis chapter 1).

Since God has a Spirit, does He also have a Soul? Several passages, including the following, reveal that answer:

- "Behold **My Servant**, whom I uphold; **Mine Elect**, in whom **My Soul** delighteth; I have put **My Spirit** upon Him: He shall bring forth judgment to the Gentiles." **(Isaiah 42:1)**

The above passage from (Isaiah 42:1) also exhibits the Trinity in the same verse. It refers to Jesus as God's Servant and God's Elect in whom the Father's Soul delights. These Scriptures illustrate how God has two of the three entities (Soul and Spirit) that fashion man's framework. The question is, was there a third entity present when God said, "...let us make man in Our image?"

Chapter 7
Satan's Ultimate Intent

We can feel confident that Satan achieved his objective in the Garden by enticing man to sin. Yet, was that his only purpose? That answer requires insight into what other schemes Satan had in mind when he beguiled Eve. When God granted dominion authority over all the earth to man, Adam became responsible for all worldly matters. In essence, God instructed him, "…to be fruitful and multiply; to replenish the earth and keep and dress the garden." There were no restrictive commandments with specific conditions attached. God did not require Adam to choose right from wrong or good from evil. He could very much do as he pleased.

Everything seemed well for Adam until God told him he could eat of every tree in the Garden, except the tree of the knowledge of good and evil. That marked the first time God gave Adam a command with a restriction. Yet, this directive had a penalty attached. If he ate of this particular tree, he would surely die. However, that is not all. The condition and the consequence added another first-time concern. Embedded within this command was man's ability to choose right from wrong and pinpoints where the man received his free will.

For the first time, a life or death decision confronted Adam. The free will provided him the power to abstain from or partake of the forbidden fruit and, if the latter was his choice, he must pay the punishment—death. God made this command to Adam alone; before He formed Eve from the rib. She could partake of the fruit, and all would be well. However, she offered it to Adam, and he ate. Thereby, Satan achieved his primary goal of bringing about sin, but that was only part of his plan.

God's Sovereignty:

When God created man, He established specific directives for him to follow. Since God made man in His image and likeness and placed him in such high authority on earth, the rules relating to man are firm. Yet, those regulations were not meant to afflict but guide us into a fulfilled life through obedience. When sin invaded the heart of Adam, it triggered a series of events. Because God is sovereign, He had the absolute power and capacity to intervene and restore the man to Himself—no questions asked. However, in doing so, He would have intruded upon the very directives He set into place. Among other things related to man, those directives declared, **"The soul that sinneth, it shall die."** (Ezekiel 18:4), and **"The wages of sin is death..."** (Romans 6:23). Another issue to ponder is; if God merely forgave Adam's sin and restored him to righteous standing before the fall, what would the rest of us do? Would someone else disobeyed God at another point in time—then what?

The Result of Violated Law:

Satan was familiar with the consequences of disobeying God because he once held a high position among the ranks of the angels. Therefore, he was fully aware of God's laws, as well as God's integrity. He knew God holds firm to His word, and by deceiving Adam and Eve, Satan not only enticed them into sin but also achieved his ultimate goal—to seize the earthly dominion. This significant phenomenon came about when Adam disregarded God's directive. Adam no longer remained obedient to God but assumed allegiance to Satan. What resulted from this act continues to haunt man even to this day. As it happened, another precept was violated, which placed the man under the control of Satan. The following Scriptures will shed light on this principle:

- "Jesus answered, Verily, I say unto you, Whosoever committeth sin is the servant of sin." **(John 8:34)**
- "Know ye not that to whom ye yield yourselves servants to obey, his servants ye are to whom ye obey; whether of sin unto death or of obedience unto righteousness?" **(Romans 6:16)**
- "He that committeth sin is of the devil;" **(1 John 3:8)**

Humanity's Dilemma:

Disobeying God's commandment, and yielding to Satan's deception, transferred man's dominion authority to Satan. In the exchange, man became a servant to both sin (John 8:34) and Satan (1 John 3:8). This one act of disobedience to God created an appearance of hopelessness. Not only did sin bring forth death, but also humanity essentially became a slave to Satan. These circumstances made any probable restoration back to God seem incredibly impossible.

Humanity Doomed:

Since Adam had no children before the fall, there were no other sinless people around. All of Adam's future descendants must also acquire his sinful nature. That plight placed them in the same situation as Adam. Without a person available to deliver man from his despair, it meant humanity was in serious trouble. Satan was in control of the dominion authority, and the *fallen man* was under the influence of the *fallen angel*.

The father of Lies:

The following Scripture bears witness to the fact that man transferred his loyalty from God to Satan:

- "**Ye are of *your* father the devil**, and the lusts of your father ye will do: he was a murderer from the beginning, and abode not in the truth, because there is no truth in him. When he speaketh a lie, he speaketh of his own: for he is a liar, and the father of it." **(John 8:44)**

When Jesus said, "Ye are of your father the devil," He spoke it to the religious leaders of His day. However, He also provided a powerful revelation for the rest of us. If the religious superiors were children of the devil, where did everyone else stand? Consider this also, if Satan is our father, then God cannot be our Father.

Satan's Authority Undisputed:

Another passage confirms Satan's claim to authority. At one point, we find Satan tempting Jesus in the wilderness by offering Him all the kingdoms of the world if He would only bow down to him. Although Jesus did not give in to the temptations, He did not dispute Satan's claim to the dominion authority:

- "And the devil, taking Him up into a high mountain, showed unto Him all the kingdoms of the world in a moment of time. And the devil said unto Him, All this power will I give Thee, and the glory of them: for that is delivered unto me; and to whomsoever I will I give it. If Thou therefore wilt worship me, all shall be Thine." **(Luke 4:5-7)**

The Result of Obedience to Satan:

Herein Jesus did not give in to Satan's enticements and rebuked him with the Word of God from the Book of Deuteronomy. If Jesus had agreed to Satan's request, He would have fallen into the same trap as Adam. By submitting to Satan's temptations, Jesus would have been disobedient to His Father's will. Notwithstanding, Satan would be under no obligation to fulfill his end of the bargain since he is the father of lies and void of moral standards.

God's Answer for Man:

Adam was a perfect human being before the fall. The only remedy for restoring man to God was through another flawless human male as Adam was initially. The difficulty of the matter maintained that since all humanity traces their ancestry back to Adam, no one could qualify. Even if such an individual existed, he had to be perfect and live a life without disobeying the Father. To avoid inheriting a sin-nature, the individual must *not* have a blood connection to Adam's lineage.

Two questions refused to go away: was there anyone available anywhere, and from where would he come? The Bible states that angels also sinned since Satan once persuaded one-third of them to join his ranks. Besides, angels and beasts are ineligible because they are neither human beings nor made in God's image and likeness.

God may have been in heaven, but He was fully aware of the desperate plight of man on earth. He knew that no matter what man attempted or how much he tried, he could never find a way out of his predicament. Yet, despite man's unfaithfulness, God's love for humanity did not stop, and that was the good news because God had an answer to the problem. What was the answer, and how did God propose to accomplish His plan?

The One Ultimate Answer:

After analyzing every conceivable possibility, it turns out that there was only one genuine solution. That sole reason for hope was—God Himself. God devised a plan whereby He would come down to earth to redeem fallen man from his situation and restore him to his original state before sin. Without a perfect human existing anywhere in the universe, God indeed was the only answer to man's dilemma.

One Major Problem:

The only hope for humanity now resided in the hands of a merciful God. Yet another obstacle stood in the way. How would God be able to achieve this feat since the Bible tells us, "no man can look upon God and live" (Exodus 33:20)? That meant God could never come down to earth to live among mortal men. Even so, the Bible also tells us, "With God, all things are possible."

- "I will ransom them from the power of the grave; I will redeem them from death; O death: I will be thy plagues; O grave, I will be thy destruction: repentance shall be hid from Mine eyes." **(Hosea 13:14)**
- "For behold, the Lord cometh forth out of His place, and will come down, and tread upon the high places of the earth." **(Micah 1:3)**

Prophecies Regarding the Messiah:

Throughout the history of the Old Testament, God made predictions known to specific individuals. The first one belonged to Satan, where, in the Garden of Eden, God foretold that the woman's seed would bruise Satan's head (Genesis 3:15). God also promised a Messiah would come from Abraham, Isaac, and Jacob (Jeremiah 33:25.26), and He would be from the tribe of Judah (Isaiah 65:9). The Kingdom of this coming Messiah would be established forever upon the throne of David (Psalm 132:11) and be born in the town of Bethlehem. He would be born of a virgin and called mighty God and Immanuel (God with us). These prophecies were open for all to see, and indeed, Satan was aware of each one.

Chapter 8

The Virgin Birth

A significant prophecy recorded in the Book of Isaiah contains a sign promised by God to the king of Judah named Ahaz regarding a virgin birth:

- "Therefore the Lord Himself shall give you a sign; Behold, a **virgin shall conceive**, and bear a son, and shall call his name Immanuel." **(Isaiah 7:14)**

The word Immanuel translates in both Greek and Hebrew, meaning *God with us*. The king, named Ahaz, was of the house of David, which ties in with another Isaiah passage documented in chapter 9:

- "For unto us a child is born, unto us a son is given: and the government shall be upon his shoulder: and his name shall be called Wonderful, Counselor, The mighty God, The everlasting Father, The Prince of Peace. Of the increase of his government and peace there shall be no end, upon the **throne of David**, and upon his kingdom to order it and to establish it with judgment and with justice from henceforth even for ever. The zeal of the Lord of host will perform this." **(Isaiah 9:6.7)**

Both Scriptures point to God coming to earth in the fashion of a Human Being. They also show the connection of the Virgin Birth to God, the house and throne of David, and the Messiah, who is to rule the world. We have established that the Trinity originated in (Genesis 3:15). Therefore, it should come as no surprise to learn that the same passage also uncovers the Virgin Birth's origin. God presented this verse to Satan in the form of a prophecy concerning his seed and the woman's seed. Thus, God told the serpent:

- "...I will put enmity between thee and the woman, and between thy seed and her seed; it shall bruise thy head, and thou shalt bruise His heel." **(Genesis 3:15)**

The passage ties together the importance of the Virgin Birth in conjunction with the Trinity. A virgin or woman cannot produce a child independently since she does not possess the seed. Another note of importance in the above verse concerns the seed of the serpent. The Bible does not provide a definitive picture of the serpent seed, but credible biblical views exist. Even so, we shall not expound on them at this time, as they are involved and not necessary for understanding the Virgin Birth. Yet, we shall still deal with the seed of the woman.

What took place at the birth of Jesus is quite significant compared to what took place in the "Garden of Eden." God's strategy to redeem fallen humanity involved using a virgin named Mary and a man named Joseph. Mary and Joseph's lineages both derive from King David and the tribe of Judah. To fulfill one of the required methods to bring forth God's only begotten Son into the world necessitated using a woman to satisfy the stipulation that He belonged to the human race. Because she was a virgin, it ensured that **the vessel chosen to contain the pure Seed** was a chaste womb.

Jesus' Lineage through God:

At the right time, God chose Mary, a virgin, espoused to the man named Joseph. The angel Gabriel appeared to Mary to declare that the Holy Ghost would come upon her, and she would conceive and be with child:

- "Then said Mary unto the angel, How shall this be, seeing I know not a man?" **(Luke 1:34)**

To this, the angel replied:

- "...The Holy Ghost shall come upon thee, and the power of the Highest shall overshadow thee...." **(Luke 1:35)**

The Child she would bear would be from God, and she was to call His name Jesus. Later, the angel also appeared to Joseph with the news about the event, and as it happened, Jesus was born in the town of Bethlehem, fulfilling another prophecy:

- "But thou, Bethlehem Ephratah, *though* thou be little among the thousands of Judea, *yet* out of thee shall He come forth unto Me *that is* to be ruler in Israel; **whose goings forth have been from of old, from everlasting.**" **(Micah 5:2)**

Micah's prophetic passage is a picture of the coming Messiah, who will be ruler in Israel. The words, **"whose goings forth have been from old, from everlasting,"** indicates this passage is *not* discussing a created mortal being. Only one has no beginning, and that is God. However, as God told Moses, no one could look upon His face and live. That meant God could never come to earth in His deified nature. Thus, only Jesus, the Son of God who entered this world in the flesh, could have fulfilled this passage.

Jesus' Lineage through Man:

The Bible contains two New Testament genealogies indicated as belonging to Jesus. The first points to Joseph's lineage in the first chapter of Matthew, and the second occurs in the third chapter of Luke and belongs to Mary's ancestry. Both genealogies relate to Jesus' physical connection.

The Lineage through Joseph:

Matthew's gospel (1:1-16) chronicles Jesus' ancestry through Joseph and notes that He was a descendant of Abraham, Isaac, Jacob, Judah, and David. Verse 16 names Joseph's immediate father as a different individual named Jacob. Thus, verse 16 reads, "Jacob begot Joseph, the husband of Mary, of whom was born Jesus, called Christ." Please observe that the passage does not say that Joseph *begot* Jesus, but that he was Mary's husband, of whom Jesus was born. Therefore, Jesus became a legal descendant, heir, and son of Joseph, even though Joseph's only connection to Jesus happened through his marriage to Mary. This relationship gave Jesus the same inheritable rights as applied to Mary and Joseph's natural-born children. It also establishes Jesus' human heredity to David, Judah, Jacob, Isaac, and Abraham through Joseph's male lineage.

Since Mary's conception was of the Holy Ghost, Jesus did not derive from a human bloodline. In other words, Jesus' ancestry did not return to Adam but God. As (Romans 1:3) reports, Jesus was of the seed of David according to the flesh, but not of the blood.

That distinction afforded Him the capability of physically dying because He was of the seed of David, but not spiritually because He was of the Holy Ghost. Humanity did not need a physical link back to God, but one spiritually. The Life infused into the pure Seed by the Holy Ghost contained pure, uncontaminated blood. As a result, it qualified Jesus to fulfill the role of the only Human Being capable of restoring humanity from sin and death to a morally justified position with the Creator God.

Both Matthew and Luke's genealogies coincide with Abraham, Isaac, Jacob, and Judah to David. This awareness is significant since Scriptures declare that God shall establish the Messiah forever from the seed of David and the tribe of Judah:

- "I have made a covenant with My chosen, I have sworn unto **David My servant**, Thy seed will I establish forever, and build up thy throne to all generations. Selah." **(Psalms 89:3.4)**

- " And thou Bethlehem, in the land of **Judah**, art not the least among the princes of **Judah**: for out of thee shall He come a Governor, that shall rule My people Israel." **(Matthew 2:6)**

Mary and Joseph settled another issue by being out of the same tribe. The last chapter of the Book of Numbers states that marriages in Israel must occur between men and women of the same tribe. Mary and Joseph each conformed by originating from the tribe of Judah.

Only Luke's gospel (verse 1:5) makes any other mention of Mary's lineage. The verse documents Mary's cousin Elizabeth as originating from the daughters of Aaron. Since they were cousins, Mary also had a connection to Aaron's daughters. However, the Bible provides no other information concerning Aaron's daughters in contrast to Aaron's sons. Still, since Aaron was the first high priest in the Old Testament, the book of Hebrews refers to Jesus as the sacrifice for sin and the ultimate High Priest. Thus, Mary's relation to Aaron's daughters finds justification.

The Virgin Birth has been a sensitive topic for many years, and rightly so. How could a virgin give birth to a child? "…with God, all things are possible" (Matthew 19:26). A quick review of the Jewish wedding arrangements in the time of Jesus will help us understand how it happened.

The Virgin Birth

The Jewish Wedding:

Jewish weddings in Jesus' day differed to some extent from Gentile weddings of today. Nevertheless, they comprise of two parts, similar to the engagement of our Western culture. The first part consisted of making arrangements and agreements by the parties involved. After those affairs were in order, the bridegroom went away to prepare a place for the two to live. This episode is what the Bible refers to as the espousal or betrothal period. By all rights, the marriage between the man and woman extended into the espousal interlude. (During the espousal interval, divorce was possible, but only because of infidelity.) Everything was in place except for one more detail. When the place they were to live in was ready, the bridegroom came back for the bride, which brings us to that last item. The second part involved the actual wedding ceremony and celebration, after which time they lived together.

The angel Gabriel appeared to the Virgin Mary and said to her:
- "And behold, thou shalt conceive in thy womb and bring forth a Son, and shalt call His name Jesus." **(Luke 1:31)**
- "…the Holy Ghost shall come upon thee, and the power of the Highest shall overshadow thee: therefore also that holy thing which shall be born of thee shall be called the Son of God." **(Luke 1:35)**

Since Mary and Joseph were in the marriage's espousal period, Joseph was gone to prepare the place to live. When the angel appeared to Mary with the news, she would become the vessel to bring forth the Son of God; sometime later, Joseph found Mary to be with Child. Being a just man, Joseph would divorce her privately when the Angel appeared to him with the news that the Infant she was carrying was of the Holy Ghost.

The Necessity of the Virgin Birth:

Exploring deeper into why the Virgin Birth was so necessary to bring forth the Son of God into the world, it may benefit to consider the following two observations. This information will also help determine why it could only have occurred in the marriage's espousal period to validate this unusual event. (Bear in mind that no intimate contact would have taken place in these examples or any commandment broken because it occurred through a supernatural overshadowing of direct implantation of the pure Seed within the womb):

1.) If Mary was a single woman and still a virgin but found to be pregnant with a child, society would consider her a harlot and not qualified to bring God's Son into the world.

2.) If Mary were a virgin when the Holy Ghost overshadowed her, yet she and Joseph had already gone through the second phase of the Jewish wedding ceremony, it would mean they were fully married. That would bring into suspect the law of adultery by raising biblical issues that intimacy could have occurred before Mary was with the child of the Holy Ghost. In other words, the question in the eyes of the secular world even today would be, "was Mary really a virgin when she had the baby, Jesus?"

With these possibilities evaluated, we find that God could not consider either a single or a married woman to fulfill His purpose without raising or violating moral issues. The Jewish espousal period was of the utmost importance to the Virgin Birth. At no other time could the overshadowing event have occurred except between the wedding ceremony's first and second phases In addition, Mary provided the angel with her acceptance and permission, and Joseph consented with his approval. If the Holy Ghost's overshadowing occurred before or after the espousal interlude or if any above situations took place, it would have nullified the birth of Jesus, as well as everything else in the Old and New Testaments.

Mary's Sin Nature:
Since Mary's genealogy traces back to Adam, it indicates her blood also became contaminated. Thus, we must ask the question, "How could the pure Seed of the Holy Ghost within her womb avoid becoming infected with her contaminated blood?" Physiology is a research science designed to help us understand the structure of the body. Its studies show that the male seed introduces the blood for the infant at the fertilization interval to sustain it throughout the growth period within the womb. Furthermore, the mother's blood and the fetus's blood never intermingle throughout the entire pregnancy cycle. The placental circulatory system consists

of a fetal and maternal separation. It restricts blood interaction through a method called the placental barrier. This barrier filters the metabolic exchanges between the infant and the mother.

Although the placental barrier prevents the intermingling of the infant and mother's blood, it allows nutrition, waste filtering, chromosomes, and other gene-inheriting factors of the mother to pass through. This critical aspect, when conjoined with the Virgin Birth, justifies how Jesus fulfilled all the prophecies concerning His position as the rightful heir to the throne of David:

- "And, behold, thou shalt conceive in thy womb, and bring forth a son, and shalt call his name JESUS. He shall be great and shall be called the Son of the Highest: and the Lord God shall give unto him the throne of his father David: And he shall reign over the house of Jacob forever; and of his kingdom there shall be no end." **(Luke 1:31-33)**

As pointed out earlier, the fact that the blood and not the flesh contained the sin-nature provides further validation that the entire Virgin Birth process had to be flawless. No mere human being could have worked out such intricate details with comparable precision. Jesus had to be perfect in every way to pay the penalty to reunite us to God, and His blood had to be free of any contaminants to atone for our sins.

Chapter 9
Jesus–the Second Adam

The Child met every requirement necessary to become a human being. Unlike Adam, Jesus was not a created being. Through the Virgin Birth, He became the first human born directly of God and not made or born of a man. The following passage is what the Old Testament Book of Psalms proclaims:

- "I will declare the decree: the Lord hath said unto Me. Thou art My Son; this day have I begotten Thee." **(Psalms 2:7)**

A View of the Cross:

Jesus fulfilled all the conditions necessary to redeem fallen humanity; yet, He had a lifetime to complete His mission without dishonoring His Father. Because he existed entirely as a Human Being, it subjected Him to the same temptations and hindrances as everyone else:

- "For we have not an high priest which cannot be touched with the feeling of our infirmities; but was in all points tempted like as *we are, yet* without sin." **(Hebrews 4:15)**

In leaving His glorious estate and His majestic throne, He became obedient even to death on the cross. The Book of Isaiah provides an inconceivable portrayal of what Jesus went through to redeem fallen humanity:

- "Behold, My servant shall deal prudently, He shall be exalted and extolled, and be very high. As many were astonied at Thee; His visage was so marred more than any man, and His form more than the sons of men." **(Isaiah 52:13.14)**

- "...despised and rejected of men; a man of sorrows, and acquainted with grief: and we hid as it were *our* faces from Him; He was despised, and we esteemed Him not. Surely He hath borne our griefs, and carried our sorrows: yet we did esteem Him stricken, smitten of God, and afflicted. But He *was* wounded for our transgressions, *He was* bruised for our iniquities: the chastisement of our peace *was* upon Him; and with His stripes we are healed. All we like sheep have gone astray; we have turned every one to his own way; and the LORD hath laid on Him the iniquity of us all." **(Isaiah 53:3-6)**

This report from the book of Isaiah generates a remarkable picture of what the Lord went through as He endured the cross. Also, verse 10 says, "Yet it pleased the LORD to bruise Him; He hath put *Him* to grief: when Thou shalt make His soul an offering for sin...." God presented His only begotten Son as an offering for sin, yet it pleased God because it provided fallen humanity with a channel for restoration from his sinful nature. The reality that it gave God pleasure to become the *Way* also gives even greater assurance of His love for man.

Although the one bruised was Jesus (God's only begotten Son), He is no less a part of the same Godhead as the Father. As we progress into our study and uncover additional details of the Trinity, this matter will become more apparent. For now, we want to realize the manner and purpose of how God compensated for the wrong done by man.

His Humanity, Not His Divinity:

The frequent question is, why didn't Jesus merely tell them He was God instead of going through all the suffering? Although Jesus could perform great miracles, such as calling down fire from the sky to convince them He was God, that was not His intent. His objective involved His humanity, not His divinity. Instead, Jesus told His disciples, He could ask of the Father, and He would send down twelve legions of angels to save Him from the cross. However, the cross was the very reason He had come to earth:

- "For the preaching of the cross is to them that perish, foolishness; but unto us which are saved, it is the power of God." **(1 Corinthians 1:18)**

Jesus-the Second Adam

The purpose of Jesus coming to this earth was not to show Himself as God, but as He said, to redeem the lost sheep in the house of Israel. However, as destiny would have it, the Jewish people rejected Christ and requested putting Him to death. After Jesus ascended into heaven, God designated a man named Paul to deliver the message of grace to the Gentiles. However, God did not exclude the Jew from receiving the salvation message of grace, and as a result, everyone is eligible to receive God's deliverance from sin. Yet, the Bible tells of a time when God shall return His affection to the Jewish people, and the dispensation of grace will end.

The Final Hours:

It would be an understatement to call the final hours in the life of the Redeemer unimaginable. The punishment that Jesus endured is beyond words to describe. Satan, *the prince of this world*, was triumphant in thinking he had contained Jesus in what seemed to be His final demise. By entering into Judas (an Apostle of Jesus), Satan set up a series of events that led to the sentence of death to his Archrival (Jesus). His objective was to coerce Jesus into a rebellious situation contrary to the will of His Father.

Satan was unsuccessful when he tempted Jesus in the wilderness, and this time, he must not fail. Satan had no claim on Jesus since His bloodline did not revert to Adam. For Satan's evil scheme to succeed, Jesus needed to be disloyal to His Father.

Thirty Pieces of Silver:

Judas agreed to betray Jesus for thirty pieces of silver, thereby opening himself up to satanic control. That betrayal led to the arrest of Jesus and culminated in His eventual crucifixion upon the cross:

- "...as a lamb to the slaughter, and as a sheep before His shearers is dumb, so He openeth not His mouth. He was taken from prison and from judgment...." **(Isaiah 53:7.8)**

Soon the demonic inventor of evil would presume success was inevitable. Defeating Jesus would achieve the ultimate victory for Satan, and he would reign supreme. God's law (Numbers 23:19) decrees that assurance. Still, Satan, so accustomed to deceiving his prey and winning, forgot to allow for one minor detail: What if Jesus did not rebel against the will of His Father? In all probability, that factor did not even enter into the picture.

Defeat Appears Certain:

Jesus endured all the pain, suffering, and torture man could provide. Despite that, He carried our griefs, sorrows, and iniquities in His own body. At the same time, Satan, confident of victory, lurked in the background awaiting his chance to mock, sneer and ridicule. Jesus was on the cross, and so close to death, defeat was unthinkable for Satan:

- "And being found in fashion as a man, He humbled Himself, and became obedient unto death, even the death of the cross." **(Philippians 2:8)**

Sinless Man Forsaken:

Then, "Jesus cried with a loud voice from the cross, Eloi, Eloi, la-ma sa-bach-tha-ni? which is, being interpreted, My God, My God, why hast Thou forsaken Me?" (Mark 15:34). When He had spoken this, He bore the sins of the world upon Himself. This occurrence marked the first time Jesus called His Father, God. Recall the Scripture, "Thou art of purer eyes than to behold evil, and canst not look on iniquity..." (Habakkuk 1:13). With the weight of sin upon Him, God could no longer behold His Son. From all appearances, it looked as if His Father had abandoned Him:

- "My God, My God, why hast Thou forsaken Me? *why art Thou so far from helping Me, and from* the words of My roaring?" **(Psalms 22:1)**

Sin came with a penalty, and that penalty was the sentence of death. At death, the soul of man takes his sins to the regions of hell for distribution appropriated for his punishment. Thus, when Jesus cried out, "It is finished"; "Father, into Thy hands I commend My Spirit," He completed His mission on earth:

- "And He made His grave with the wicked, and the rich in His death; because He had done no violence, neither was any deceit in His mouth." **(Isaiah 53:9)**

Now, another mission was in the making. Jesus took the sins of the world upon Himself, but that alone did not pay the penalty. Those sins could not merely remain on Jesus—the full punishment for sin needed reparation.

Dominion over the Whole Earth:

While Jesus was on the cross, He remarked to a thief on a cross next to Him, "...Today shalt thou be with Me in paradise." Therefore, we know Jesus went to paradise the day He died. Both (Acts 2:25-31) and (Ephesians 4:9.10) disclose that Jesus descended into the lower parts of the earth, the location of hell. The possibility exists that Paradise and hell's position were both located in the lower regions of the earth, with a gulf separating the two.

In (Luke 16:19-31), we find an account of a rich man and a beggar man named Lazarus, which lay at the rich man's gate. The rich man never helped the beggar while the two were alive. The passage continues as it paints a picture of when they both died. The rich man being in torment, could see Lazarus across a vast gulf consoled in Abraham's bosom. Many scholars agree this is a look at hell and Paradise before the crucifixion. Another picture emerges after Jesus rose from the dead (Matthew 27:52.53). Here, the graves of the saints opened, and they arose and appeared to many in the city of Jerusalem. This event suggests that those in Paradise obtained freedom from the earth's center to a heavenly location. It also provides credence to (Isaiah 5:14), which declared, "Hell has enlarged itself." Other Scriptures reveal:

- "...being put to death in the flesh, but quickened by the Spirit: By which also He went and preached unto the spirits in prison." **(1 Peter 3:18.19)**
- "For as Jonas was three days and three nights in the whale's belly; so shall the Son of man be three days and three nights in the heart of the earth." **(Matthew 12:40)**
- "...Thou wilt not leave My Soul in hell, neither wilt Thou suffer Thine Holy One to see corruption." **(Psalms 16:10) (Acts 2:27)**

We conclude from these Scriptures that Jesus descended into the lower parts of the earth, to the area called hell, the place of the dead. There He deposited the sins of humanity:

- "Now that He ascended, what is it that **He also descended first into the lower reaches of the earth?**" **(Ephesians 4:9)**

Jesus endured the punishment of the cross and took our sins to the lower reaches of the earth. Satan met Him there with victory in his eyes, but divine justice demanded that the dominion authority now belonged to Jesus since He was an innocent man. That is when Satan's victory plans quickly changed.

The dominion authority applied not only to the surface but also to the whole earth. Since hell's location is in the center, it too is included as verified by Jesus who recovered the keys while in hell:

- "I am He that liveth, and was dead; and, behold I am alive for evermore, Amen; **and have the keys of hell and of death.**" **(Revelation 1:18)**

Jesus completed His mission, and Satan lost the battle. By entering into Judas and initiating the death of an innocent man (Luke 22:3), Satan himself violated a law of divine justice. As a result, Jesus invalidated Satan's legal claim to authority and established salvation for humanity. By remaining faithful unto death, His victorious conquest is undisputed. Jesus achieved complete repossession of the dominion authority:

- "Who, being in the form of God, thought it not robbery to be equal with God: But made Himself of no reputation, and took upon Him the form of a servant, and was made in the likeness of men: And being found in fashion as a man, He humbled Himself, and became obedient unto death, even the death of the cross." **(Philippians 2:6-8)**

Who Killed Christ?

Many still inquire concerning who was responsible for killing Jesus. Some blame the Jews; others blame the sinner. While the Jews did bear responsibility for the actual *crucifixion* and sinners were accountable for the real *reason*, we must note that no one person or group caused Christ's death. As (Genesis 3:15) mentioned, Satan would bruise His (Jesus') heel. We looked at the following passage earlier to explain the omission of the words Jesus and Trinity from the Old Testament, but it is also applicable in this case:

- "But we speak the wisdom of God in a mystery, even the hidden wisdom, which God ordained before the world unto our glory; Which none of the princes (demonic spirits) of this world knew: for had they known it, **they would not have crucified the Lord of glory**." **(1 Corinthians 2:7.8)**

Jesus-the Second Adam

In this passage, Paul states that the Bible omitted Jesus' name from the Old Testament for a specific reason. If the princes or demonic spirits of this world had known who Jesus was and what His purpose involved, they would not have crucified the Lord of glory. The passage's significance gives rise to the fact that although the entire human race is equally at fault, Satan and his hordes are genuinely responsible. When Judas opened his heart to betray Jesus, he opened the door for Satan to enter in and initiate the crucifixion (Luke 22:3). The name Jesus was a mystery kept secret in the Old Testament, and His mission remained hidden until after the cross. Even though the apostles heard Jesus speak of His death, they did not fully realize it until after the infilling of the Holy Ghost at Pentecost. They thought Jesus would set up His Kingdom on earth in (Acts 1:6).

In His first coming, He became Redeemer and Savior. When He comes the second time, He will reign as Lord of lords and King of kings.

Exposing Satan:

The evil one is now defeated, but that does not stop his attacks. He knows that Jesus is the only way to salvation and attempts everything in his power to hinder the proclamation of the gospel. How does he do this? He uses the sinner man who continues as a slave under his bondage.

Unlike God, Satan cannot be everywhere at once, but the fallen angels are still under his dominance, doing his dirty work throughout the earth. Working steadfastly, they go about deceiving those who are willing and vulnerable.

The Bible states that even the devils believe, and they tremble. They understand the fate of their future and the closeness of the hour. Although he could not defeat Jesus, Satan's clear objective is to take as many with him as possible.

The Bible again asserts that Satan sometimes masquerades as an angel of light. Jesus declared that Satan only comes to steal, kill, and destroy. He *stole* the dominion authority from man, he was responsible for the *killing* of Jesus, and he wants to take humanity to the same *destruction* in store for him:

- "For we wrestle not against flesh and blood, but against principalities, against powers, against the rulers of the darkness of this world, against spiritual wickedness in high *places*." **(Ephesians 6:12)**

Jesus defeated Satan in his own game plan. Truth overcame lies; good overcame evil; life overcame death, righteousness overcame wickedness, and love overcame hate. Not only that, but Jesus said the gates of hell shall not prevail against His Church to whom He gave all authority over the wiles of the devil.

Summary of Chapter 9:

This chapter reveals the love God has for man. God devised a way to redeem man back to Himself. In a sense, Jesus became the second Adam and suffered all the grief and agony man could bestow upon Him. Yet, He overcame it all and regained access for our redemption. However, although Jesus recovered the dominion authority, it did not erase man's freedom to choose.

Chapter 10
What the Cross Fulfilled

For a savior to fulfill his purpose, there must be someone with a need and a desire to be saved. We have determined that everyone needs a Savior, but the apparent reality concludes, not everyone possesses the desire. With that in mind, let us probe into what the cross did and did not accomplish by redeeming humanity.

The cross and its victory over Satan create the appearance of automatic deliverance from sin and its consequences. However, this is simply not the case. Even though Jesus lived a sinless life without obtaining a sin-nature and died for the sins of the whole world, the structure of man did not change. In effect, nothing changes until an individual decides to transfer their allegiance from Satan back to God. Jesus regained the dominion authority, but our inherited sin-nature allows Satan to continue to influence us in temptations and trespasses. As long as a sin-nature is prevalent in our lives, Satan can always manipulate our shortcomings. He may be incapable of reading our mind, but he can observe the things that sway our tendencies toward the sins that so easily beset us.

Sowing to the Flesh:
The flesh remains the main hindrance in the process of receiving salvation. The body's attributes significantly influence our daily lives and consume much of our daily thoughts and concerns. As a rule, we desire to keep the outer-man in the best operating condition possible by providing much time and effort toward achieving that goal.

Even though the flesh consumes much of life's endeavors, Jesus said, "It is the Spirit that quickeneth; the flesh profiteth nothing" (John 6:63). The writer of Ecclesiastes also made a notable comment when he summarized his findings of life. After checking out the things done under the sun, he concluded with these three words, "All is vanity." The following two passages make a distinction between attempting to reach God through Adam's lineage (sin and the flesh) or Jesus' sacrifice (the Spirit):

- "For if ye live after the flesh, ye shall die: but if ye through the Spirit do mortify the deeds of the body, ye shall live." **(Romans 8:13)**
- "For he that soweth to his flesh shall of the flesh reap corruption; but he that soweth to the Spirit shall of the Spirit reap life everlasting." **(Galatians 6:8)**

Knowledge of God:

Separation from the Spirit of God does not mean God completely removed His Spirit from our being, but that our soul is void of life. As established earlier, God's Spirit lives within each one of us, and therefore, we are without excuse:

- "For the invisible things of Him from the creation of the world are clearly seen, being understood by the things that are made, even His eternal power and Godhead, so that they are without excuse." **(Romans 1:20)**

The Offering for Sin:

Divine justice still demands payment for the penalty of sin (Romans 6:23). If Jesus had not taken our sins and deposited them in hell, they would be in His possession today. The following Scriptures verify that Jesus no longer carries those sins:

- "So Christ was once offered **to bear the sins of many**; and unto them that look for Him shall He appear the second time **without sin** unto salvation." **(Hebrews 9:28)**

Notice what (Hebrews 9:28) declares. Christ was once offered to bear the sins of many (not all), and to those who look for Him shall He appear. However, when an individual rejects the salvation provided through Christ, the penalty for sins remain unpaid:

- "Therefore they say unto God, Depart from us; for we desire not the knowledge of Thy ways." **(Job 21:14)**

That means when an individual rejects God's pardon for his sins; he must eventually make payment for them himself. When an individual decides to pay for his own sins, it also expresses his desire to keep Satan his master. At the death of such an individual, Satan becomes his master for eternity, including inheriting all his benefits, namely: death, hell, and the grave:

- "He that committeth sin is of the devil; for the devil sinneth from the beginning…." **(1 John 3:8)**

No Changes in Man's Framework:

In examining man's structure one more time, we find his composition did not change after the cross:

1. The principles of the body, soul, and spirit utilize the same functions as before.
2. The bloodline extends back to Adam—lacking the capacity to reconnect to God.
3. He retains his sins and the potential to sin by using his acquired knowledge of good and evil.
4. Freedom of choice and separation from God's Spirit still exists after the cross, as before the cross.
5. Despite everything, the punishment for sin remains as before— the penalty of death. So what purpose did the cross serve?

The Individual's Choice:

It is now possible to regain access to the dominion authority seeing that Christ recovered it from Satan. Yet, sometimes Satan's enticements hinder an unsaved person from his desire to accept Jesus. However, once they make the choice, the truth will set them free:

- "Forasmuch then as the children are partakers of flesh and blood, He also Himself likewise took **part** of the same; that through death He might destroy him that had the power of death, that is, the devil;" **(Hebrews 2:14)**

Before the cross, we were limited to one choice: Satan and death. The cross of Calvary provided another option in that by recognizing the triumph of the cross and Christ as the One who fulfilled it; we now have the power to become sons of God:

- "But as many as received Him, to them gave He power to become the sons of God, *even* to them that believe on His name:" **(John 1:12)**

Man is also a trinity, existing in body, soul, and spirit. His inherited relationship back to Adam is both physical and spiritual. However, death occurs in both cases. A passage in (1 Corinthians 15:45) describes Jesus as the last Adam, which shows that the way back to God is spiritual, "The first man Adam was made a living soul, the last Adam (Jesus) was made a quickening Spirit." However, the first Adam *became* a dead soul through disobedience, and the last Adam continued as a quickening Spirit through obedience.

When Jesus met the woman at the well in (John 4:24), He disclosed, "God is a Spirit." He also told us that the flesh profits nothing, but the Spirit gives life. Therefore, our objective is to reach God spiritually, not physically. Putting these truths in their proper perspective will help us see what purpose the cross *did* serve.

The Cross Became a Shortcut:

Primarily, the cross serves as a bridge or shortcut back to God. He led a sinless life as a Man, making it possible to become a child of God, and thereby breaking our **spiritual ties** to Adam's ancestry:

- "For as many as are led by the Spirit of God, they are the sons of God." **(Romans 8:14)**

Changes Made Through the Cross:

When we choose salvation over sin, our heritage makes a significant turnabout. Adam's ancestry is no longer an obstacle in our pursuit to reach God. Jesus' accomplishment on the cross provides direct access to God. Our spirit receives life through the Spirit of God, and the blood of Jesus cleanses us from all unrighteousness. We no longer yield ourselves as slaves to sin, but as Jesus said, "If the Son shall make you free, ye shall be free indeed." This simpler ancestry breaks our bondage to Satan, with our roots restored to God. Disobedience initiated separation from God, but acceptance reunites us with God. Deliverance assures that bondage to Satan ceases, and although trials and temptations shall occur as before, Satan's authority over us ends, but our dominance over Satan begins.

Chapter 11
The Born-again Experience

Born-again is another unique Christian concept, yet the expression appears only twice in the New Testament. The first happening occurs in the third chapter of John's gospel and the other in Peter's first epistle. Different related biblical terms include "born of God" and "children of God."

The New Birth:
Some have a hard time accepting the realism of the word Born-again. Even so, only the ones who have experienced this phenomenon can justify its truth. In the third chapter of John's gospel, Jesus made a significant statement to Nicodemus, a ruler of the Jews. As the two walked by night, Jesus revealed details concerning the requirement for an individual to enter into the Kingdom of God. Jesus said to Nicodemus, "Except a man be born-again, he cannot see the kingdom of God" (John 3:3). Nicodemus asked, "Can a man be born when he is old?" Jesus answered, "Except a man be **born of water** and of the Spirit, he cannot enter into the kingdom of God." Then Jesus defines the water and the Spirit by stating, "that which is **born of the flesh is flesh**, and that born of the Spirit is spirit." The wording of these verses has spawned several trains of thought as to their meaning. However, a closer look at "born of water" and "born of the flesh is flesh" renders the same purpose and comprises the same substance, which is physical.

In verse 8, Jesus, speaking of the wind listing where it comes from and where it goes, added this, "so is every one that is **born of the Spirit**." There is no further mention of water or flesh. In simple terms, that born of the flesh is physical, and that born of the Spirit is spirit. As much as everyone is born from the womb, only those who receive Jesus as their Lord and Savior are born spiritually.

Nicodemus was unable to understand what Jesus meant by the term *born-again*. However, we are not in the dark as we read more of the Gospels and other Scriptures, which help formulate what *born-again* means.

The first epistle of Peter expands on the phrase as he provides this description:

- "**Being born again**, not of corruptible seed, but of incorruptible, by the Word of God, which liveth and abideth for ever." **(1 Peter 1:23)**

The Wrong Path:

Man's natural instinct seeks to satisfy his spiritual hunger. He senses a void within his heart but is unable to reason what or why. Without God's Spirit to fill man's spirit with life, he impulsively searches for anything connected with a spiritual tone attached. If it impresses him, he will usually follow it, sometimes without wise judgment. More often than not, religion is the way he chooses to fill the void. The bad news is—there are many paths available for him to venture, each claiming to be the right one:

- There is a way that seemeth right unto a man, but the end thereof *are* the ways of death." **(Proverbs 14:12)**

Renovating the Soul:

When an individual encounters a new-birth experience, a transforming change takes place. Therefore, it would be fitting to gain awareness of how this happening operates and what it entails.

Earlier, we mentioned that a baby or small child is too young to recognize sin because knowledge of good and evil does not resonate within him or her. Only when a child reaches the age of accountability and realizes right from wrong and acts on it does sin occur. At the point of transgression, the child becomes accountable and must become *born-again*.

The Gospel Preached to Everyone:

The following passage reveals that everyone has heard the gospel:

- "...be not removed away from **the hope of the gospel** which ye have heard, and which was **preached to every creature** which is under heaven;" **(Colossians 2:23)**

The Wide and Narrow Roads:

Jesus said; there are only two roads in this life. Each road leads to a specific destiny. There is no middle road, and only you can choose the route for your journey:

- "Enter ye in at the strait gate: for wide is the gate, and broad is the way, that leadeth to destruction, and many there be which go in thereat: Because strait is the gate, and narrow is the way, which leadeth unto life, and few there be that find it." **(Matthew 7:13.14)**

Not Through the Law:

To many whom Jesus healed, He said, "Go thy way, thy faith has made you whole." He did not mention that the law has made you whole, but faith. However, the epistle of James says that "if we should keep the whole law and yet offend in one point, we are guilty of all—for there is no difference in one point over the other." So what good is the law? Paul tells us it is our schoolmaster to bring us to Christ. Paul added, "Is the law sin? God forbid, Nay, I would not have known sin, but by the law; for if righteousness come by the law, then Christ is dead in vain."

- "Therefore, by the deeds of the law there shall no flesh be justified in His sight: for by the law is the knowledge of sin." **(Romans 3:20)**
- "Knowing that a man is not justified by the works of the law, but by the faith of Jesus Christ...." **(Galatians 2:16)**

Only One Place:

The Scriptures reveal that there is only one place to find salvation. The following verse concerns the Lord Jesus and declares:

- "Neither is there salvation in any other: for there is none other name under heaven given among men, whereby we must be saved." **(Acts 4:12)**

Grace, Works, and the Law:

Here is the result of the (spiritual) sin-nature each individual carries within their (physical) blood:

- "For all have sinned, and come short of the glory of God;" **(Romans 3:23)**
- "**For the wages of sin is death**, but the gift of God is eternal life, through Jesus Christ our Lord." **(Romans 6:23)**

Grace is the righteousness of God. Scripture says, "There is none righteous, no, not one." Thus, we cannot be righteous through ourselves because of our sin-nature. However, by believing in the Lord Jesus Christ, God takes us where we are and what is in our hearts. No works are involved, and no requirement to be perfect or belong to a particular religion. The Bible says, "For whosoever shall call upon the name of the Lord shall be saved" (Romans 10:13).

God Desires Salvation for All:

How does God feel about someone rejecting salvation? The following Scriptures give us an idea:

- "Have I any pleasure at all that the wicked should die? saith the Lord God: *and* not that he should return from his ways, and live?" **(Ezekiel 18:23)**
- "The Lord is not slack concerning His promise, as some men count slackness; but is longsuffering to us-ward, not willing that any should perish, but that all should come to repentance." **(2 Peter 3:9)**
- "For God sent not His Son into the world to condemn the world; but that the world through Him might be saved." **(John 3:17)**

The Encounter:

This passage, written by Paul to the Roman church, records the simplicity of the born-again experience:

- "If thou shalt confess with thy mouth the Lord Jesus, and shalt believe in thine heart that God raised Him from the dead, thou shalt be saved. For with the heart man believes unto righteousness; and with the mouth confession is made unto salvation." **(Romans 10:9.10)**

Acknowledging the need for Jesus indicates the desire for salvation. Confessing Jesus as Lord and believing God raised Him from the dead meets the new birth requirements. This action allows God to take over on His part. Our part initiates the desire for salvation.

The Born-again Experience

John's gospel records this statement of Jesus, "No man can come to Me, except the Father which hath sent Me draw him..." (John 6:44). Somehow, an awakening of an individual's spirit must occur before the Father draws that someone to Jesus. The Bible provides several observations of how this might happen, including the following:

- One way is by hearing the Word of God. "Faith comes by hearing, and hearing by the Word of God" (Romans 10:17). Thus, drawing attention to God's Word is one way a person is attracted to Jesus.
- The prayers of *born-again* individuals can encourage the heart of an unsaved individual. A passage from (James 5:16) states, "...The effectual fervent prayer of a righteous man availeth much."
- Another way to arouse the heart toward salvation is through the witness of a Christian believer who will share the gospel message and pray with that one to receive Christ into their life.

The Trinity at Work:

There is no requirement to believe in the Trinity to become *born-again*, but it suffices to say that it is obtainable only through the workings of God's Triune nature. In the following passages, we see the beneficial workings of the Trinity within the confines of salvation:

- Jesus said, "I am the Way, the Truth and the Life, no man cometh to the Father, but by Me." **(John 14:6)**
- "And I will pray to the Father, and He shall give you another Comforter, that He may abide with you for ever." **(John 14:16)**
- "...He that raised Christ from the dead shall also quicken your mortal bodies by His Spirit that dwelleth in you." **(Romans 8:11)**

The New Life:

Within the 10-seconds it takes someone to call upon the name of the Lord, the Spirit of God takes up residence within the heart for eternity. Thus, the term *born-again* finds its meaning:

- "...after that ye believed, ye were sealed with that Holy Spirit of promise." **(Ephesians 1:13)**

An epistle of Peter calls them peculiar people, called out of darkness into His marvelous light. Another passage adds this description:

- "Therefore if any man be in Christ, he is a new creature: old things are passed away; behold all things are become new." **(2 Corinthians 5:17)**

The guidance of the Spirit imparts the desire to serve God, which takes precedence over serving sin:

- "There is therefore now no condemnation to them which are in Christ Jesus, who walk not after the flesh, but after the Spirit." **(Romans 8:1)**

In our first birth, we take on the physical traits of our earthly parents. In the New Birth, we take on our heavenly Father's spiritual characteristics through the workings of the Holy Spirit. Whereby our physical birth inherits the sin-nature, in essence, the "Born-again" experience takes us back to Adam's right standing with God before he sinned.

Chapter 12
Messiah and Prophecies

The Book of (Genesis 3:8) hints that God walked with man in the Garden, but the walks ended after Adam's transgression. From that point forward, God's focus centered mainly on the redemption of humanity. To reach that objective, God chose a man named Abraham. At one hundred years of age, Abraham fathered a son named Isaac. That event fulfilled a promise of God. Later, when Isaac was a child, God told Abraham to sacrifice Isaac. By faith, Abraham willingly obeyed. However, God prevented the sacrifice from happening, and Abraham's faith became the basis for salvation.

Through Abraham, His son Isaac, and Isaac's son Jacob, God established a covenant. In effect, the promise ushered in Israel's birth, which became the apple of God's eye and His chosen nation. After becoming slaves in Egypt, God sent a man named Moses to the Hebrew people to set them free from their bondage. During this time, God gave Moses the Ten Commandments. Jewish history records times of obedience and rebellion toward God, and for the most part, God displayed compassion on them. Try as they may, the commandments were impossible to keep.

Overlooked—the Need for a Savior:
Scattered throughout the Holy Scriptures were the promises of a coming Messiah (Redeemer), yet confusion existed because the Savior was to come to earth twice. Many leaders among the Jewish nation could not distinguish between the various Scripture passages and only saw a one-time coming of this Redeemer.

When the Savior finally arrived, word of His ministry spread rapidly, and within a short time, many became His followers. Even so, many others departed when they realized He taught a different message than the one delivered by the religious. The following passage might provide a clue for their leaving. John's gospel offers a capsule of what Jesus talked about while speaking to a crowd regarding the death He was to experience:

- "And I, if I be lifted up from the earth, will draw all *men* unto Me. This He said, signifying what death He should die. The people answered Him, **We have heard out of the law that Christ abideth for ever:** and how sayest Thou, The Son of man must be lifted up? who is this Son of man?" **(John 12:32-34)**

This passage reveals that their Messiah would come to earth in the Jewish teachings, but only once. As these verses declare, they heard out of the law that Christ was to come, and when He did, He would abide forever. What they failed to realize was that He must first come to redeem fallen humanity.

The Scheme Seemed Right:

This erroneous understanding had to make Satan happy since it fit into his scheme. He was glad, that is until he realized what he had done by killing an innocent Man. Christ's crucifixion also had to make the religious happy because Jesus quit preaching against their doctrine. Yet, it also fits into the design of an all-knowing God, but it must have hurt Him intensely to see it happen. Nevertheless, God restored His children to Himself, and the love of God now shines forth in the hearts of those who love Him. Jesus could not have assumed our place at death unless He paid the total price for our redemption.

Guilt and Denial:

Another difficulty occurred because of what happened at Calvary. The crucifixion of an innocent man not only won our release but also placed a guilt trip on the Jewish people. Their rejection of Jesus as their Messiah also made salvation available to the nations just as God promised Abraham. The result—Jew and Gentile alike have received God's gift of eternal life during this time of grace.

Messiah and Prophecies

Old Testament Prophecies:

The Old Testament contains many prophecies concerning both the First and Second Coming of the Messiah. Astoundingly, the New Testament fulfilled all those relating to Messiah's first coming. We have listed some Old Testament prophecies concerning the First Coming and some for His Second Coming:

They Shall Call Him:
- "For unto us a child is born, unto us a Son is given: and the government shall be upon His shoulder: and His name shall be called Wonderful, Counselor, The mighty God, The everlasting Father, The Prince of Peace." **(Isaiah 9:6)**
- "Of the increase of *His* government and peace *there shall be* no end, upon the throne of David, and upon His kingdom, to order it, and to establish it with judgment and with justice from henceforth even for ever. The zeal of the Lord of hosts will perform this." **(Isaiah 9:7)**

Out of Bethlehem:
- "But thou, Bethlehem Ephratah, *though* thou be little among the thousands of Judah, *yet* out of thee shall He come forth unto Me *that is* to be ruler in Israel; whose goings forth *have been* from of old, from everlasting." **(Micah 5:2)**

The Promise of the Messiah:
- "Behold the days come, saith the LORD, that I will raise unto David a righteous Branch, and a King shall reign and prosper, and shall execute judgment and justice in the earth. In His days Judah shall be saved, and Israel shall dwell safely: and this is His name whereby He shall be called, **THE LORD OUR RIGHTEOUSNESS**." **(Jeremiah 23:5.6)**

Time of His Arrival:
- "Know therefore and understand, *that* from the going forth of the commandment to restore and to build Jerusalem unto the Messiah the Prince *shall be* seven weeks, and threescore and two weeks: the street shall be built again, and the wall, even in troublous times." **(Daniel 9:25)**
- "And after threescore and two weeks shall Messiah be cut off, but not for Himself: and the people of the prince that shall come

shall destroy the city and the sanctuary; and the end thereof *shall be* with a flood, and unto the end of the war desolations are determined." **(Daniel 9:26)**

The Messenger to Prepare the Way:
- "Behold, I will send My messenger, and he shall prepare the way before Me: and the Lord, whom ye seek, shall suddenly come to His temple, even the Messenger of the covenant, Whom ye delight in: behold, He shall come, saith the Lord of hosts." **(Malachi 3:1)**

Prophecies and Their Fulfillment:
The prophecies of the first coming include several about the crucifixion and death of Christ on the cross. The passages below contain more Old Testament prophecies along with their fulfillment in the New Testament:
- "Rejoice greatly, O daughter of Zion; shout, O daughter of Jerusalem: behold, thy King cometh unto thee: He *is* just, and having salvation; lowly, and riding upon an ass, and upon a colt the foal of an ass." **(Zechariah 9:9)**
- "And they brought the colt to Jesus, and cast their garments on Him; and He sat upon him." **(Mark 11:7)**

* * * * * * * * *

- "I gave My back to the smiters, and My cheeks to them that plucked off the hair: I hid not My face from shame and spitting." **(Isaiah 50:6)**
- "Then did they spit in His face, and buffeted Him; and others smote *Him* with the palms of their hands." **(Matthew 26:67)**

* * * * * * * * *

- "All they that see Me laugh Me to scorn: they shoot out the lip, they shake the head, *saying*, He trusted on the Lord *that* He would deliver Him: let Him deliver Him, seeing He delighted in Him." **(Psalm 22:7.8)**
- "And the people stood beholding. And the rulers also with them derided *Him*, saying, He saved others; let Him save Himself, if He be Christ, the chosen of God." **(Luke 23:35)**

* * * * * * * * *

- "They gave Me also gall for My meat; and in My thirst they gave Me vinegar to drink." **(Psalms 69:21)**

- "They gave Him vinegar to drink mingled with gall: and when He had tasted *thereof*, He would not drink." **(Matthew 27:34)**

* * * * * * * * *

- "He keepeth all His bones: not one of them is broken." **(Psalm 34:20)**
- "But when they came to Jesus, and saw that He was dead already, they brake not His legs:" **(John 19:33)**

* * * * * * * * *

These were but a few of the Old Testament prophecies concerning the coming of the Jewish Messiah. The predictions and the eyewitness accounts provided by the Apostles offer a powerful combination to consider.

The Disciples and the Messiah:

The notion the Messiah would die was not in the teachings of the Jews. He was a coming Savior, but also a King: not someone spat upon and humiliated. Even His disciples abandoned Him when the soldiers took Him captive. Yet, His resurrection and appearance in the glorious body with the nail prints caught them unaware because they never truly understood His purpose.

We must remember these men were also Jews. They knew of the Messiah and the expectations of His one-time coming to earth. They just recently witnessed the triumphant entry of Jesus into Jerusalem. At that time, they thought they would crown Him King of kings. No wonder they could not understand when Jesus talked about His death. No wonder they fled when the soldiers captured Jesus. In their way of thinking, the Messiah would be a Redeemer, not taken to prison and put to death.

Jesus appeared several times to His disciples within the 40 days that He remained on earth after the resurrection. These manifestations confirmed their conviction that Jesus was beyond a doubt the Messiah. Then came the day they watched Him ascend into the heavens. That experience in itself was enough to convince anyone who Jesus was, but ten days after the ascension, the Holy Ghost came to dwell in their hearts. Together these happenings produced more than enough evidence to settle that Jesus is indeed God in the flesh.

How did the Apostles recall what they recorded in the New Testament? A promise made by Jesus assured them that the Holy Ghost would bring to remembrance the things He said and did while on earth. In this way, the Apostles were able to formulate the writings for the New Testament:

- "But the Comforter, *which is* the Holy Ghost, whom the Father will send in My name, He shall teach you all things, and bring all things to your remembrance, whatsoever I have said unto you." **(John 14:26)**

Summary of Chapter 12:

This chapter substantiates that the Trinity is not just a New Testament concept. Throughout the Old Testament, God told of the coming Messiah. However, man took control of the teachings and made them fit his agenda. Therefore, after man added his version, the Truth was lost. The result—the people missed the first coming and even crucified their Messiah.

Chapter 13
Issues Surrounding the Trinity

The first biblical mention of the word Christian occurs in the eleventh chapter of Acts. Today, many sects and cults use the Christian classification because the name Jesus fits somewhere within their dogma. It is fitting to know that Paul warned about those who preached another gospel than what he preached (Galatians 1:8). Due to the universal uncertainty of the Trinity, false information continues to surface concerning God's Triune nature. Most matters of difficulty come from *misunderstanding* the Scriptures. This chapter shall offer a sampling of questions to clarify some disputes confronting the Trinity and its related doctrines. We shall also look at a matter of inconsistency within Christianity itself.

Questions and Debates:
Since the first coming of Christ, many have attempted to understand the Trinity. It seems beyond natural reasoning to envision someone in the form of a Human Being, yet not from Adam's lineage. To compound matters, this Person is also God. Thus, those endeavoring to discredit the Scriptures and the Trinity must warn others that Jesus is not really who He said He is. While some believe that Jesus did exist, they cannot accept the fact He is also God. Let us look at some biblical difficulties with those thoughts in mind, which certain factions express as false teachings.

The Voice and Shape of God:
The following Scripture is one focal point of confusion by some non-Christians. From this one verse, many have justified a motive for rejecting the Trinity:

- "And the Father Himself, which hath sent Me, hath borne witness of Me. Ye have neither heard His voice at any time, nor seen His shape." **(John 5:37)**

Here we have Jesus talking to a group of Jews who sought to persecute and slay Him because He healed a man on the Sabbath day. This single verse is only one of several that make up the whole passage. In it, Jesus provides an answer to Jewish accusations. The skeptic's concern here is how Jesus can also be God when the people looking at Him see His shape and hear His voice.

Their reasoning seems credible when first encountered, but we shall find that misunderstanding the Trinity is the root of the problem. Remember, Jesus dwelt in a human physical body, not a spiritual body. God is a Spirit and is in heaven. Of a truth, Jesus was speaking the words of God. Despite that, His voice did not sound like God's voice but that of the human form He inhabited. Likewise, His shape was not a spirit form, but as of a human being. For a picture of the voice of God, we must go to the Book of Exodus:

- "And all the people saw the thunderings, and the lightnings, and the noise of the trumpet, and the mountain smoking: and when the people saw *it*, they removed, and stood afar off. And they said unto Moses, Speak thou with us, and we will hear: but let not God speak with us, lest we die." **(Exodus 20:18.19)**

We can conclude from this passage that God's voice is so overwhelming to hear it could cause death. The same also applies to see God's shape as depicted in this next verse:

- "And He (God) said, Thou canst not see My face: for there shall no man see Me, and live." **(Exodus 33:20)**

This passage renders a portrait of God, but not in a human form, as with Jesus. It is God in His Spirit form. Yes, God allowed Moses to glance at His backside, but this was because Moses requested to look at Him. Although he did not see God's face, the event did cause Moses to glow to the extent he needed to wear a veil over *his* face. The thunderous voice of the Father would frighten even the bravest human. To look upon God in His Spirit form would cause immediate death.

The Difficulty in Confirming His Deity:

Another notable hindrance to those who oppose the Trinity is this, "If Jesus were God, why didn't He just come right out and say so?" This idea also sounds like a valid question until we consider the following. It is essential to recognize that regardless if Jesus would have told them time and again He was God and, despite everything, confirmed His deity with great signs and miracles, what justification would it have produced? Chances are they would not have crucified Christ, and in so doing, would have defeated the very purpose for His coming to earth—that purpose was to redeem fallen humanity.

Jesus Performed Miracles and Healing:

On the other hand, didn't Jesus do many works of miracles such as changing water into wine, raising the dead, and all manners of healing? To answer this question, we must consider that no one knew the whole story before His crucifixion. Even the Apostles did not understand until after the resurrection, and even then, not entirely. They only became aware of their calling after the Holy Ghost fell upon them in the upper room. Even today's standards, it would be unwise to follow someone who claimed he was a prophet sent by God without any evidence but his word. There was something about Jesus that made these men leave everything they had and immediately follow Him.

So why did Jesus do the works that He did? Jesus answered this question Himself. He did them because, even if they did not believe in Him for who He was, at least they could for His work's sake (John 14:11). Bear in mind that if Jesus had not performed any healing and miracles, many even today would question His deity. However, we must also remember that His followers were eyewitnesses to the works and saw them first hand. Without these followers, what good would it do if no one else knew about the redemptive plan of salvation? For this reason, they saw what He did, they believed what He said, and they proclaimed the same message throughout the land. Thankfully, this is the same salvation message of grace through faith being shared throughout the world today.

The Promise of the Holy Ghost:

Even more remarkable was the promise of the third Person of the Trinity. After Adam fell to sin in *the Garden*, the Holy Spirit never reconnected with the heart of man in the Old Testament. The prophets of old were righteous men, inspired, and filled with wisdom and knowledge by the Holy Ghost. However, redemption only came by way of Jesus, who paved the way for a Pentecost moment. It made the availability possible for all to become children of God. The prophets of old prophesied of the day when God *would* pour out His Spirit.

On the day of Pentecost, Peter gave this account, "But this is that which was spoken by the prophet Joel; And it shall come to pass in the last days, saith God, I will pour out of My Spirit upon all flesh..." (Acts 2:16.17) (Joel 2:28). Ezekiel reports this, "And I will put My Spirit within you..." (Ezekiel 36:24-28).

Jesus assured us that He would send His Holy Spirit to those who accept Him as Lord. Jesus cannot be everywhere because He exists today in a Human form. However, the Holy Spirit *is* omnipresent and available to each individual. It is by the promise of the Holy Ghost that we have the guarantee of our salvation (Ephesians 1:13.14).

Jesus a Prophet Like Moses:

Another problematic passage for non-Christians comes from the Old Testament. Moses remarked to the Israelites that "The Lord thy God will raise up unto thee a Prophet from the midst of thee, of thy brethren, like unto me; unto Him ye shall hearken;" (Deuteronomy 18:15). The contention here is that Moses was a man, and the coming Prophet whom God would raise up would be a man like unto Moses. This rationale seems logical until we consider Jesus begotten directly from God and not created.

While Jesus was a Prophet like Moses, He was not a man like Moses. Moses was born to his father named Amram. The Israelites were also slaves in Egypt, and Moses was the one who saves them. This contrast is but a shadow of the Prophet, which was to come. As Moses led the Israelites from slavery through the wilderness to *the Promised Land*, so Jesus leads us out of slavery to sin through this earthly journey to *the Promise Land*. We find this assessment verified and fulfilled in the following passage:

- "For Moses truly said unto the fathers, A Prophet shall the Lord your God raise up unto you of your brethren, like unto me; Him shall ye hear in all things whatsoever He shall say unto you. And it shall come to pass, that every soul, which will not hear that Prophet, shall be destroyed from among the people." **(Acts 3:22.23)**

Dual Meanings:

Although few exist, some Scripture passages could possess a dual meaning. Conflicts may arise when only one side of the inference is evident. For example, (Hosea 11:1) contains such a passage, which refers to Israel. However, (Matthew 2:15) alludes to the same reading as referring to Jesus. Which is right? To study the Word correctly, we must accept that they both fit appropriately and find out why:

- "When Israel was a child, then I loved him, and **called my son out of Egypt**." **(Hosea 11:1)**
- "And (Jesus) was there (in Egypt) until the death of Herod: that it might be fulfilled which was spoken of the Lord by the prophet, saying, **Out of Egypt have I called my son**." **(Matthew 2:15)**

Mary, the Mother of God?

This issue is a matter of contention within Christianity. It deals with the conviction regarding Mary as the mother of God. Perhaps more evident than any is the tradition of reciting the rosary by repeating the phrase, "***Holy Mary, mother of God**, pray for us sinners....*" Considering God and the extent of His existence, it is inappropriate to justify a mortal being created by God, from Adam's lineage, referred to as God's mother. Yet, this teaching is one taught to many since childhood.

The Bible indicates that Mary raised Jesus and kept Him until He was ready to be on His own. She did everything expected of a mother in rearing a child. The Bible mentions that Mary and Joseph were married for at least twelve years—the age of Jesus when He was lost and found teaching in the temple. Indeed Mary and Joseph would not have gone through twelve years of marriage without intimacy, and the Bible also hints Joseph was alive near the time of Jesus' crucifixion (John 6:42). If intimacy did occur, Mary ceased being a virgin. The Bible reports that Jesus had several brothers and sisters, and specific passages mentioned the brothers' names: (Matthew 12:46, Matthew 13:55, Mark 6:3, Luke 8:19, John 2:12, Acts 1:14).

Another passage states, "Mary shall be called blessed," and nothing can minimize her position of honor for being the one chosen. Yet, was she the mother of God as some still profess and teach? Yes, she was the mother of His humanity. Did Mary, whose genealogy extends back to Adam (Luke 3:38), give birth to God? If she was an offspring of Adam, it makes sense she also needed a Savior. In actuality, she acknowledged her need for a Savior in (Luke 1:47), where she declared, "And my spirit rejoices in God my Saviour."

Perhaps a better question would be, "Is it *wrong to* **believe** Mary to be the mother of God?" I would think not since some scholars cannot provide a proper explanation. However, there is a real danger, and it exists in Mary's glorification. Scripture is clear—worship belongs to God alone (Isaiah 42:8).

The Issue of Sin:

What has sin to do with the Trinity? Everything, considering it initiated Trinity's necessity. The Bible describes sin as the transgression of the law (1 John 3:4). We conclude from Scripture that all have sinned and come short of the glory of God (Romans 3:23). The Bible does not differentiate between transgressions, as evident in the following passages:

- "For whosoever shall keep the whole law, and yet offend in one *point*, he is guilty of all. For He that said, Do not commit adultery, said also, Do not kill. Now if thou commit no adultery, yet if thou kill, thou art become a transgressor of the law." **(James 2:10.11)**
- "If we say that we have no sin, we deceive ourselves, and the truth is not in us. If we confess our sins, He is faithful and just to forgive us *our* sins, and to cleanse us from all unrighteousness." **(1 John 1:8.9)**

Someone who never encountered *the new birth* has never made Jesus their Lord. Therefore, the only real quality a non-believer has is his sin-nature, which we have already established operates from the flesh. The only way to rid the soul of the stain of sin is by washing it in the blood of Jesus.

Does that mean God does not love the sinner? By realizing the actual reason for the cross was to save sinners, that question is without merit. God is love and loves all humanity. Good or bad, He still loves us. A better question might be, does the sinner love God? The Bible discloses our sins will find us out. We cannot escape God even when we try to blot Him out of our minds. Psalms 139:8 reports, "If I ascend up into heaven Thou *art* there: if I make my bed in hell, behold, Thou *art there*."

On the one hand, we find justice demanding payment for sin; on the other, mercy offers a ransom. There is no other option.

- "If the righteous scarcely be saved, where shall the ungodly and the sinner appear?" **(1 Peter 4:18)**

A Look at Hell:

Salvation is an excellent choice considering the alternative. Nevertheless, temptations so easily entice us to desire this world's attractions. While the Bible speaks much about hell, perhaps Jesus provides an observable view of what it entails and why we would want to avoid the place:

- "If your hand (or eye) offends thee, cut it off (pluck it out): it is better for thee to enter into life maimed, than with two, to go into hell, into the fire that never shall be quenched. Where their worm dieth not, and the fire is not quenched." **(Mark 9:43-48)**

Consider also the following passage from the Book of Revelation chapter 20. It speaks of a Great White Throne Judgment whereby "...death and hell delivered up the dead which was in them: and they were judged every man **according to their works,** and they were cast into the lake of fire..." (Revelation 20:13.14).

Rejecting God for sinful pleasures means there is a price to pay. Yet, in all this, we can be sure that God does not send anyone to hell; it falls back on the free will.

Chapter 14
The Humanity of Christ

The focal point of this chapter is to show the human qualities of Jesus and answer the question, "How is the cross of 2000 years ago able to make salvation available for mankind today?" To gain knowledge of this and broaden our understanding of the Trinity, we want to look at certain happenings after Jesus' resurrection. First, the Bible details the reaction of the disciples after Jesus rose from the dead. Yet, if that event was not remarkable enough, consider an equally astounding sight only a few weeks later. To set the stage for this incident, we must turn our attention to one particular Scripture verse. In this report, we find that Jesus scarcely finished relaying His final instructions to His Apostles before ascending into heaven. The Bible provides the following picture of this spectacular event as it unfolded:

- "And when He had spoken these things, while they beheld, He was taken up; and a cloud received Him out of their sight." **(Acts 1:9)**

They Watched Him Go Up:
We find something of specific interest within this verse of Scripture. When Jesus ascended into heaven, they beheld Him as He departed upward. Seeing Him and watching as He rose out of sight discloses that He went up in whole Body, Soul, and Spirit. Why is this important? Seeing and watching Him go up out of their sight reveals, He was in a human form and not a spirit form. If He had inhabited a spiritual framework when He ascended, the apostles would not have been able to see Him go up. If Jesus returned to heaven in only a spiritual body and assumed the same

elevated position He occupied before becoming human, it would have nullified salvation for everyone. Perhaps if we consider the following two passages, it will help provide a better understanding.

Die Once:

In the book of Hebrews, we find the following statement:

- "And as it is appointed unto men once to die, but after this the judgment." **(Hebrews 9:27)**

In this passage, we discover that man dies only once. In other words, we do not come back to pass away again. Being a Man, Jesus was subject to all the laws concerning man, indicating He could only die once for our sins. Thus, there was no second chance for humanity's redemption.

Dust to Dust:

This next verse reveals a statement God made to Adam before banishing him from the *Garden of Eden*:

- "In the sweat of thy face shalt thou eat bread, till thou return unto the ground; for out of it wast thou taken: **for dust thou art, and unto dust shalt thou return.**" **(Genesis 3:19)**

This Scripture declares that the body of man returns to the dust of the ground. Although Jesus was in human form, He did not go back to the earth because He was not *from* dust. Jesus was born directly of God, and, as is the case with a mortal man, the body of Jesus returned to where it came from, and that was heaven.

Flesh and Blood in Heaven:

Because Jesus went into heaven bodily, another passage confronts us to investigate, but from a different perspective. "Now this I say, brethren, that flesh, and blood cannot inherit the kingdom of God; neither doth corruption inherit incorruption" (1 Corinthians 15:50). Notice that this passage explicitly mentions flesh *and* blood, not flesh *or* blood. Being aware of this detail helps as we look at other events that transpired after the resurrection. We shall revisit this matter concerning flesh and blood again shortly. Our aim now is to illustrate how and why Jesus, even to this day, remains in a human form. Yes, it is a glorified form, meaning it is void of any blood; yet, still fashioned of a living human being.

The Humanity of Christ

Why is this important? If Jesus reclaimed the same divine position He employed before His incarnation, His redemptive efforts would have been in vain. The door of salvation would have shut for humanity. By ascending into heaven in a visible body, means Jesus retained His status as a Man. As stated, the Savior had to be as Adam was before he sinned because only a perfect human being could redeem sinful humanity. For that reason, salvation remains in effect for everyone by way of a sinless Human Being. Now let us explore some passages regarding Christ's humanity, both before and after His ascension.

Jesus Retained His Deity:
Our first impression might be that Jesus had to relinquish his divinity as God to retain His humanity, but that is not the case. He continues to maintain His divinity in the same fashion after the crucifixion as before. A separation between the Father and Son could only deem possible when Jesus took upon Himself the sins of the world. When Jesus cried out, "My God, My God, why hast Thou forsaken Me," separation did not genuinely occur. Despite all appearances, it was not that the Father had turned away from Jesus, but from the sins, He bore.

If the Father did abandon the Son, Jesus would still have Life within Himself. That was the promise given to Him by the Father (John 5:26). Even so, this marked the first time the Father could not behold the Son. We may perceive it in the following manner—the attachment was there, but not the embrace. Once Jesus deposited the sins and paid the penalty, the embrace returned, allowing the Father to raise Him from the dead (Acts 4:10).

Jesus Appears to His Disciples:
At another special event right after the resurrection, we find the disciples gathered, conversing about Jesus and how He had appeared to some of them. While they were yet talking, Jesus appeared in their midst. They became frightened and terrified and supposed they had seen a spirit. Jesus said to them, "Why are ye troubled? and why do thoughts arise in your hearts? Behold My hands and My feet, that it is I Myself: handle Me, and see; for a spirit hath not **flesh and bones**, as ye see Me have. And when He

had thus spoken, He showed them His hands and His feet. And while they yet believed not for joy, and wondered, He said unto them, Have ye here any meat? And they gave Him a piece of a broiled fish, and of an honeycomb. And He took it, and did eat before them" (Luke 24:36-43).

This passage makes it evident Jesus was in a bodily form when He visited the Apostles. There is no reason to doubt that the blood, which Jesus spilled out at Calvary through His body and the holes in His hands, feet, and side, issued forth any more blood. It would even be sufficient to say that Jesus no longer retained any blood in His entire body. This analysis agrees with the report from the verse above in (Luke 24:36-43) where Jesus reveals He was not a spirit, but His Body consisted of **flesh and bone**. It helps to realize they did not readily recognize Him in this passage. We also find similar unawareness occurrences in other passages after He rose from the dead because He dwelt within a glorified Body.

Added Justification:

To validate our findings, consider another Scripture found in (1 Timothy 2:5) yielding this evidence, "For there is one God, and one mediator between God and men, the **Man** Christ Jesus." This reference to Jesus as a Man supports the reality that He resides in Heaven in His humanity. Not only that, but this verse, which states Jesus is the one mediator between God and man, also justifies a statement of Jesus in (John 14:6), "...no man cometh unto the Father, but by Me." Consequently, only through Jesus can we have direct access to the Father. Because Jesus continues to retain His humanity assures to this very day that salvation remains accessible to everyone. Jesus continues as the perfect Human Being and is seated at the Father's right hand (Acts 7:56) as the only mediator between God and man.

The Disciples and the Promises:

For nearly three years, the apostles and disciples followed Jesus. They watched, they listened, and they learned all the things He said and did. To make sure that they understood who He was, Jesus revealed Himself to them after His resurrection. Seeing Jesus in the flesh made them realize that of truth, He was the Son of God. It also encouraged the fact that they must set the Great Commission as their number one priority. Man must be aware that redemption exists and know how to receive it.

After Jesus ascended into Heaven, His disciples were the ones left to continue with the work of announcing the Good News. They obtained everything necessary to carry out the commission. Jesus did His part—now it was up to His followers to continue the assignment. Jesus taught them firsthand and brought those things into their remembrance as He promised. With revelation from the Holy Spirit, they composed and transcribed the inspired works of the New Testament and boldly proclaimed the Gospel message throughout the land.

There was one other promise Jesus made before He left earth. He departed, giving the assurance He would return for them and everyone who believes in Him as their Lord:

- "In My Father's house are many mansions: if it were not so, I would have told you. I go to prepare a place for you. And if I go and prepare a place for you, I will come again, and receive you unto Myself; that where I am, there ye may be also." **(John 14:2.3)**

Blood in Heaven:

Now let us re-examine the issue of flesh and blood in heaven. We referred earlier concerning two particular passages: flesh **and** bone, the other: flesh **and** blood. As we established, Jesus went into heaven in a body of flesh **and** bone. However, (1 Corinthians 15:50) passage states that flesh **and** blood cannot enter heaven. Thus, the expected conclusion is that no blood exists in heaven; but the fact is, blood does reside in heaven. However, this blood is not within any flesh, but upon the vesture worn by Jesus as the following passage affirms:

- "...heaven opened, and behold a white horse, and He that sat upon him was called Faithful and True, and in righteousness He doth judge and make war. His eyes were as a flame of fire, and on His head were many crowns; and He had a name written, that no man knew, but He Himself. And **He was clothed with a vesture dipped in blood**: and His name is called The Word of God." **(Revelation 19:11-13)**

Since Jesus resides in heaven in a body of flesh and bone, it does not contradict (1 Corinthians 15:50). The blood found upon the vesture is not contradictory either because it is not present within the flesh. This blood is the same shed by Jesus on the cross—the unstained and uncontaminated blood covering sin. Everything concerning a natural man's corruptible flesh and blood is consistent with what we studied in the earlier chapters about the body, soul, and spirit. For a mortal man to enter into the Kingdom of heaven, he must also attain a glorified body. The next verse discloses the way it happens:

- "Behold I show you a mystery; We shall not all sleep, but we shall all be changed, In a moment, in the twinkling of an eye, at the last trump: for the trumpet shall sound, and the dead shall be raised incorruptible, and we shall be changed. For this corruptible must put on incorruption, and this mortal *must* put on immortality." **(1 Corinthians 15:51-53)**

The picture of Jesus clothed in a vesture dipped in blood (Revelation 19:11-13) illustrates Jesus ready to return to earth as King of kings and Lord of lords. This blood is indeed the untainted covering provided for all time by Jesus for our sins. This passage demonstrates the Age of Grace is over, and Jesus is preparing to return to earth with those called the Church. Thus, the vesture will also return with Him. This passage points to the reign of Christ on earth for a thousand years, and the blood covering must therefore play a role on earth during that period. In addition, the same passage also identifies where the religious leaders, who misread the Scriptures, were looking for their Messiah. They neglected to foresee the need for a Savior and the necessity for salvation from bondage to sin.

The Nail Prints:

The Jewish people handed down the denial of Jesus as the Messiah from one generation to the next. While the rejection persists, one must only turn to the Old Testament to verify the truth. For Jesus to ascend bodily into heaven indicates that the nail prints are still visible in His body. The 22nd Psalm notes this evidence as follows:

- "For dogs have compassed Me: the assembly of the wicked have enclosed Me: they have **pierced My hands and My feet.**" **(Psalm 22:16)**

The Humanity of Christ

Much of the 22nd Psalm is a picture of Jesus as He hung on the cross. This single verse indicates the nail prints He received from His crucifixion. Other Old Testament passages also tell of the wounds of the Messiah:

- "And I will pour upon the house of David, and upon the inhabitants of Jerusalem, the spirit of grace and of supplications: and they shall look upon **Me Whom they have pierced**, and they shall mourn for Him, as one mourneth for his only son, and shall be in bitterness for Him, as one that is in bitterness for his first-born." **(Zechariah 12:10)**
- "And one shall say unto Him, **What are these wounds in Thine hands**? Then He shall answer, Those with which I was wounded in the house of My friends." **(Zechariah 13:6)**
- "But He was **wounded** for our transgressions, He was bruised for our iniquities: the chastisement of our peace was upon Him; and with His stripes we are healed." **(Isaiah 53:5)**

The above passages portray the Messiah as pierced and wounded. Notice too, Trinity's second Person speaking as God in **(Zechariah 12:10)**.

The Son of God Depicted in the Old Testament:
- "I will declare the decree: the Lord hath said unto Me, **Thou art My Son**; this day have I begotten Thee." **(Psalms 2:7)**
- "Kiss **the Son**, lest He be angry, and ye perish from the way, when His wrath is kindled but a little. Blessed are they that put their trust in Him." **(Psalms 2:12)**
- "Who hath ascended up into heaven, or descended...Who hath established the ends of the earth? What is His name, and what is **His Son's name**, if thou canst tell?" **(Proverbs 30:4)**
- "...Lo, I see four men loose, walking in the midst of the fire, and they have no hurt: and the form of the fourth is like **the Son of God**." **(Daniel 3:35)**

Summary of Chapter 14:
This chapter illustrated the importance of the bodily ascension of Jesus into heaven. We have realized our objective, confirming that Jesus remains in His Human form. Although His deity formulated our redemption, His humanity secured it. Yet, He did not discard His divine nature to retain His humanity. Instead, even to this very day, He is entirely God and fully Man. That means His nail-scarred hands and feet are still visible today in heaven.

Chapter 15
The Holy Spirit

Practically every Book of the Bible mentions the third entity of the Godhead, and thus far, we have touched upon several of those references. A commonly asked question concerns what capacity the Holy Spirit serves in the Trinity. The easy answer is many and varied. However, Jesus alluded that the primary reason is to guide the believer in holiness and worship. He told His disciples He would send them a Comforter, the Spirit of truth; whom the world cannot receive because it seeth **Him** not, neither knoweth **Him** (John 14:16.17). In this context, the Holy Spirit is the believer's connection to Jesus while He has gone back with His Father.

Some have inquired about the proper way to address the Holy Spirit from a biblical viewpoint. The Bible lists several passages, including the one mentioned above in (John 14:16.17), which refers to the Holy Spirit as **Him**. Another report from (Acts 8:16) concerns Peter and John praying for some men to receive the Holy Ghost. The verse states, "For yet **He** (the Holy Ghost) was fallen upon none of them...." This verse makes it apparent that the Holy Ghost is a Person distinguished as **He**. Another question regards the Holy Ghost's equality with God. Here a different Scripture from the book of Acts provides the answer; "But Peter said, Ananias, why has Satan filled thine heart to lie to the Holy Ghost..., thou hast not lied unto men, but unto **God**" (Acts 5:3.4). Therefore, this passage recognizes the Holy Ghost as **God**.

John 14:26 references the Holy Ghost as the Comforter, which in the Greek is called parakletos. This word means helper, intercessor, or advocate, an accurate description of several biblical terms applicable to His various positions in the Godhead.

The third Person of the Trinity is not far from any of us as Jesus advises how much more God will give His **Holy Spirit** to them who but ask Him (Luke 11:13).

Jesus Warns us:
- "...All manner of sin and blasphemy shall be forgiven unto men: but the blasphemy of the **Holy Ghost** shall not be forgiven unto men, And whosoever speaketh a word against the Son of man, it shall be forgiven him: but whosoever speaketh a word against the **Holy Ghost**, it shall not be forgiven him, neither in this world, neither in the world to come." **(Matthew 12:31.32)**

God is a Spirit:

Genesis 1:2 provides the first mention of God's Spirit, where He moved upon the face of the waters in the Creation. Generally, when the Bible speaks of God, it is referring to the Father. However, when Jesus was talking to a woman at the well, He presented something notable about the Father:

- "But the hour cometh, and now is, when the true worshippers shall worship the Father in spirit and in truth: for the Father seeketh such to worship Him. **God *is* a Spirit**: and they that worship Him must worship *Him* in spirit and in truth." **(John 4:23.24)**

This passage enlightens us that God is a Spirit. Although we already knew this fact, it permits us to get a picture of God's Spirit dwelling in man. Bear in mind that Jesus became God's only begotten Son. While God has only one begotten Son, He has many *born-again* sons and daughters. Although God's Spirit can dwell within the hearts of many, it is nonetheless one Spirit. We find a representation of this in the gospel of Matthew where Jesus is talking to His followers:

- "But when they deliver you up, take no thought how or what ye shall speak: for it shall be given you in that same hour what ye shall speak. For it is not ye that speak, but **the Spirit** of your Father which speaketh in you." **(Matthew 10:19.20)**

The Holy Spirit

Obviously, for the Spirit of the Father to speak in you and through you, His Holy Spirit must first be living in you. These Scriptures refer to those who have received salvation, and it opens up the possibility of restoring every man, woman, and child to their intended state of fellowship with God. Those who received salvation also acquire God's Spirit. This action portrays that the Spirit of God remains one Spirit, even though He resides within the hearts of many. This phenomenon is the omnipresence of God highlighted in the following passage:

- "There is one body, and **one Spirit**, even as you are called in one hope of your calling; One Lord, one faith, one baptism, One God and Father of all, who is above all, **and in you all**." **(Ephesians 4:4.5)**

Personal Concerns of the Holy Spirit:

- "Wherefore I give you to understand, that no man speaking by the Spirit of God calleth Jesus accursed: and that no man can say that Jesus is the Lord, but by the Holy Ghost." **(1 Corinthians 12:3)**
- "Know ye not that ye are the temple of God, and that the Spirit of God dwelleth in you?" **(1 Corinthians 3:16**
- "This I say then, Walk in the Spirit, and ye shall not fulfill the lust of the flesh." **(Galatians 5:16)**
- "And grieve not the Holy Spirit of God, whereby ye are sealed unto the day of redemption." **(Ephesians 4:30)**

Names and Offices of the Holy Ghost:

The following are some names and tasks designated to the Holy Spirit:

Anointer - (Isaiah 61:1); (Luke 4:18); (Acts 10:38)
Baptizes - (Matthew 3:11); (Acts 1:5); (Acts 11:16)
Comforter - (John 14:16); (John 14:26); (John 16:7)
Father - (Matthew 10:20); (Luke 11:13); (John 15:26)
Fruits of the Spirit - (Galatians 5:22.23)
Giver of Gifts - (1 Corinthians 12:7-11)
God - (Genesis 1:2); (Matthew 3:16); (Acts 5:3.4)
Sanctifier - (Romans 15:16); (1 Corinthians 6:11)
Teacher - (John 14:26); (1 John 2:27)

Provisions of the Holy Spirit:
He guides us in prayer.
He stirs up our faith.
He builds up our boldness.
He reveals the Word.
He is our hotline to the Father.
He is our comforter when we feel depressed.
He is our lawyer when we are in trouble.
He is our peace when we need some rest.
He melts the heart of the sinner.
He anoints us in ministry.
He convicts us of our wrong.
He sets the captives free.

The Gifts of the Holy Spirit:
- "For to one is given by the Spirit the word of wisdom; to another the word of knowledge by the same Spirit; To another faith by the same Spirit; to another the gifts of healing by the same Spirit; To another the workings of miracles; to another prophecy; to another discerning of spirits; to another divers kinds of tongues; to another the interpretation of tongues: But all these worketh that one and the selfsame Spirit, dividing to every man severally as he will." **(1 Corinthians 12:8-11)**

The Fruit of the Spirit:
- "But the fruit of the Spirit is love, joy, peace, longsuffering, gentleness, goodness, faith, meekness, temperance: against such there is no law." **(Galatians 5:22.23)**

Who Hath Taught Him?
- "Who hath directed the Spirit of the Lord, or being His counselor hath taught Him?" **(Isaiah 40:13)**

Many offices designated for the Father are also relevant for the Son and the Holy Spirit. Many names and offices about the Trinity are interchangeable. This chapter's significance is to reference some of the Holy Spirit's purposes and demonstrate that the Trinity does not separate God into three different people but all work together to achieve a common goal.

Chapter 16
Declarations of His Deity

We have previously looked at the humanity of Jesus. In this chapter, we shall browse through some passages concerning His deity. The gospels mention Jesus as the only **begotten** Son of God. Many agree that His earthly ministry began at His baptism, where the approval of the Father and anointing of the Holy Spirit took place. Immediately following that event, the Spirit led Him into the wilderness where He fasted for forty days, being tempted by the devil. Jesus then began proclaiming the Kingdom of God and the need to repent and believe the gospel. It did not take long for His fame to spread throughout the region. At one point, the religious sent officers to capture Him. The account they brought back summarized the authority and wisdom by which Jesus spoke. In their report, the officers replied, "Never man spake like this Man" (John 7:46). Even though His ministry progressed bountifully—eventually, He developed His audience mainly around His disciples. His purpose was to prepare Himself and the followers for the death He was about to endure.

Scriptures Relating to His Deity:

A passage from Matthew's gospel exhibits a demonstration of Jesus' divinity. The Scripture concerns a man sick with palsy lying on a bed. Jesus was in the process of healing the man and said to him, "... Son, be of good cheer; thy sins be forgiven thee. And, behold, certain of the scribes said within themselves, This *man* blasphemeth. And Jesus knowing their thoughts said, Wherefore think ye evil in your hearts? For whether is easier, to say, Thy sins be forgiven thee;

or to say, Arise, and walk? But that ye may know that the Son of man hath power on earth to forgive sins, (then saith He to the sick of the palsy,) Arise, take up thy bed, and go unto thine house. And he arose and departed to his house" (Matthew 9:2-7).

While Jesus did not directly say He was God, the things He said, and did, gave them evidence. In essence, Jesus had the authority to heal the man of the palsy by saying thy sins be forgiven or take up your bed and walk. Both cases encompassed forgiving his sins and curing the disease.

To establish other evidence of Jesus' deity while on earth (Exodus 34:14) maintains that worship belongs to God alone. Yet, angels, shepherds, wise men, and others adored Jesus. He had power over the wind and the sea (Matthew 8:26), authority over demons (Luke 4:34.35), and supremacy over diseases (Luke 4:39). The following passages provide other details verifying His deity.

His Angels and His Kingdom:
- "The Son of man shall send forth **His angels**, and they shall gather out of **His kingdom** all things that offend, and them which do iniquity;" **(Matthew 13:41)**

The angels and the Kingdom belong to Him.

Jesus Acknowledges He Is Christ:
- "... Again the high priest asked Him, and said unto Him, Art Thou the Christ, the Son of the Blessed? And Jesus said, **I am**: and ye shall see the Son of man sitting on the right hand of power, and coming in the clouds of heaven." **(Mark 14:61.62)**

The Messiah:
Jesus told the woman He met at the well He is the Messiah:
- "The woman saith unto Him, I know that **Messias** cometh, which is called Christ: when He is come, He will tell us all things. Jesus saith unto her, **I that speak unto thee am *He*.**" **(John 4:25.26)**

Jesus' Relationship with His Father:
Next, we want to look at some passages relating to Jesus' relationship with His Father and position in the Godhead.

The Importance of Acknowledging Jesus as Lord:
- "Whosoever therefore shall confess Me before men, him will I confess also before My Father which is in heaven. But whosoever shall deny Me before men, him will I also deny before My Father which is in heaven." **(Mathew 10:32.33)**

Giving Honor:
- "All *men* should honour the Son, even as they honour the Father. He that honoureth not the Son honoureth not the Father which hath sent Him." **(John 5:23)**

The Son is to receive the same honor as the Father.

Sent to do Father's Will:
- "For I came down from heaven, not to do Mine own will, but the will of Him that sent Me." **(John 6:38)**

His Equality:
- "I and *My* Father are one." **(John 10:30)**

The Only Way:
- "I am the Way, the Truth, and the Life, no man cometh to the Father, but by Me." **(John 14:6)**

Bold Statements:
Jesus also made many statements concerning His position in the Godhead and His claim to salvation. He placed humanity on notice that they must accept or deny what He said as truth by making these claims.

The Result of Believing:
- "Verily, verily, I say unto you, He that believeth on Me hath everlasting life." **(John 6:47)**

The Result of Not Believing:
- "I said therefore unto you, that ye shall die in your sins: for if ye believe not that I am *He*, ye shall die in your sins." **(John 8:24)**

More Passages Concerning His Deity:
- "Jesus cried and said, He that believeth on Me, believeth not on Me, but on Him that sent Me. And he that seeth Me seeth Him that sent Me." **(John 12:44.45)**
- "Jesus saith unto him, Have I been so long time with you, and yet hast thou not known Me, Philip? he that hath seen Me hath seen the Father; and how sayest thou *then*, Show us the Father?" **(John 14:9)**

- "Neither pray I for these alone, but for them also which shall believe on Me through their word; That they all may be one; as Thou, Father, *art* in Me, and I in Thee, that they also may be one in Us…." **(John 17:20.21)**

The passages presented in this chapter represent only a portion of those that testify of Jesus' deity. Yet, even though they testify of His deity, He was in human form when He made the statements. That certainly opened the door for a room full of doubt in the heart of the hearer and could have been reason enough for the outcry to crucify Him when that time came.

Chapter 17
The Revelation of the Trinity
(Part 1 - The Covenants)

Over the years, the shrouded image of the Trinity has generated more questions than answers:
1. How did the Father reside in heaven while the Son was on earth?
2. Is Jesus really God's only Son?

In time, these questions proved challenging because no one could provide practical answers. Lacking clarification of the Trinity directly added to the confusion. To settle the issue, they labeled the Trinity a mystery and concluded the matter resolved. Still, this identity was not for lack of answers in the Bible, but that God had withheld the revelation from us until these last days.

The Trinity's primary intent is to generate new life into a sin-filled soul destined for an eternity of death and hell. However, this new life does not manifest itself with empty words but with life-changing proof of God's Spirit active within the heart of the believer:

- "If the Spirit of Him that raised up Jesus from the dead dwell in you, He that raised up Christ from the dead shall also **quicken your mortal bodies by His Spirit that dwelleth in you**." **(Romans 8:11)**

The 12th chapter of Daniel foretold that as we progressed toward the end, knowledge would increase. Today, God is confirming fulfillment of Daniel's prophecy as we see advancements in all areas of society, especially in the technological fields. However, not only is this knowledge reserved for the secular populace, but it also supports the Trinity and answers that seemingly problematic question (Deuteronomy 6:4) regarding how the LORD our God is One LORD.

Laying Out the Puzzle Pieces:

Throughout Scripture, we find God methodically laying out His overall design for humanity. From Adam's sin in the Garden to the woman's seed in (Genesis 3:15), it seemed God had His master plan under control. The only thing necessary was to lay out all the puzzle pieces and bring everything to fruition. God made several covenants with man throughout the time required to fulfill His plan. Those agreements were vital for Trinity's overall purpose.

One such pact was a covenant made through Noah to the future earthly inhabitants that He would not destroy the earth again with water of a flood. As a token of this covenant, He would place a rainbow in the clouds for all to see. Although this pledge to Noah does not affect the Trinity, we will now look at four other covenants that directly impact revealing the mystery.

The Abrahamic Covenant:

It seems God wasted no time in implementing His redemptive plan as recorded in (Genesis 3:15) concerning the seed of the woman. Yet, it was nearly 2000 years later before the next event came into play. This time, to bless all the nations and call out a separated people unto Himself, God chose a man named Abraham to carry a seed.

Abraham, originally known as Abram, fathered a child named Ishmael by Hagar, the maidservant of Abram's wife, Sarai. However, Ishmael was not the promised seed that Abram was to carry because God changed Abram's name to Abraham and changed his wife Sarai's name to Sarah right before giving birth to Abraham's son Isaac.

The purpose of changing Abram and Sarai's names was to ensure no one could mistake through whom the Abrahamic covenant evolved. If Ishmael were to be the one through whom the promise came, it would have been "the Abramic" covenant. God also pledged the same agreement He made with Abraham to Abraham's son Isaac and Isaac's son Jacob.

The covenant was a twofold pledge. In the first part, God set the Hebrew nation of Israel apart for Himself. This part of the promise indicated that the Jewish people would increase in multitude with the assurance of everlasting possession of the land of Canaan:

- "I will give to thee and to thy seed after thee, the land wherein thou art a stranger, all the land of Canaan **for an everlasting possession**; and I will be their God." **(Genesis 17:8)**

The other part declared blessings on all the nations of the world through the seed of Abraham:

- "And in thy seed shall all the nations of the earth be blessed: because thou hast obeyed My voice." **(Genesis 22:18)**

This covenant embodies Abraham's faith exhibited in his obedience to God when he willingly went through the motions of sacrificing his son Isaac on an altar before an angel stopped him. Thus, Abraham's faith ushered in the age of grace for the nations:

- "And God brought Abraham forth abroad, and said, Look now toward heaven, and tell the stars, if thou be able to number them: and He said unto him, So shall thy **seed** be." **(Genesis 15:5)**
- "And I will make thee exceedingly fruitful, and I will make nations of thee...." **(Genesis 17:6)**

The Mosaic Covenant:

Several years later, God raised a man named Moses to lead the Hebrew people out of slavery in Egypt to the land of promise. God performed many miracles along their journey to the new nation, but the people grumbled, complained, and disobeyed along the way. Therefore, God gave Moses a set of laws and commandments for the Jewish people to abide by (Exodus Chs. 19&20). Also, God gave them conditions determined by their obedience to those commands. The Book of Deuteronomy chapter 28 contains a detailed list of blessings and curses disbursed according to their ways.

The Davidic Covenant:

Years later, God raised a man named David, whom God called: "a man after My own heart, which shall fulfill all My will." As a youth, David slew the giant named Goliath. After David became the king, God decreed to him a covenant (2 Samuel 7:8-17). God promised to establish the throne of **David's seed** forever:

- "And when thy days be fulfilled, and thou shalt sleep with thy fathers, I will set up **thy seed** after thee, which shall proceed out of thy bowels, and I will establish His kingdom." **(2 Samuel 7:12)**

The following passage records another occurrence of the promise:

- "Behold, the days come, saith the Lord, that I will raise unto David a righteous Branch, and a King shall reign and prosper, and **shall execute judgment and justice in the earth**. In His days Judah shall be saved, and Israel shall dwell safely: and this is His name whereby He shall be called, **THE LORD OUR RIGHTEOUSNESS." (Jeremiah 23:5.6)**

So there is no mistaking the identity of "**the One who will execute judgment in the earth,**" we find this from the Book of Micah:

- "But thou Bethlehem Ephratah, though thou be little among the thousands of Judah, yet out of thee shall He come forth unto Me that is to be **ruler in Israel; whose goings forth have been from old, from everlasting**." **(Micah 5:2)**

This event happens when the one from the seed of David sets up His Kingdom upon the earth. He is the One the Jewish rulers were looking for at Jesus' First Coming.

The New Covenant:

The three preceding covenants ushered in the way for a better promise called "The New Covenant" (Jeremiah 31:31-34). This covenant would be different from the rest in that God would write His laws upon their hearts, and they would worship and obey God in spirit and truth. Thus, Abraham's seed, the commandments made known to Moses, and David's seed are all fulfilled within this covenant or awaiting completion at His Second Coming (Hebrews 8:6-13). The following New Testament passages provide references to show how God fulfilled the three Old Testament covenants.

Abrahamic Covenant Fulfilled:

The nation of Israel came about when the Hebrew populace came out of bondage in Egypt, entered in, and conquered those who inhabited the land that God had promised them. However, the New Testament's age of grace happened when the Jewish people rejected Paul's testimony concerning Jesus as their Messiah. After the rejection, Paul and other Church leaders preached Christ to the Gentiles and the Jews who would listen to their message. This occurrence fulfilled the blessing of the nations that God promised to Abraham.

Abraham received the promise of the seed first, and it became the basis for the physical attributes of Jesus. Luke's gospel links Abraham to Mary's genealogy, and Matthew's gospel relates him to Joseph. The passage below contains a reference to Christ as the seed of Abraham:

- "Now to Abraham and his seed were the promises made. He saith not, And to seeds, as of many; but as of one, And to thy **seed, which is Christ.**" **(Galatians 3:16)**

Mosaic Covenant Fulfilled:

The Mosaic covenant included the commandments, the blessings, and the curses. In this New Covenant, Jesus did not do away with the law but fulfilled it. That means it did not disappear but is still in effect for those who desire to live under the law. For those longing to live under grace, Christ fulfilled the law and wrote it within their hearts. Today, God offers this grace through faith to all:

- "Think not that I am come to destroy **the law**, or the prophets: I am not come to destroy, but to fulfill." **(Matthew 5:17)**
- "For sin shall not have dominion over you: for ye are not under the law, but under grace." **(Romans 6:14)**

Since Jesus *fulfilled* the law, Mary and Joseph's genealogies do not list Moses as a descendant because there is no seed in the law.

Davidic Covenant Fulfilled:

- "Concerning His Son Jesus Christ our Lord, which was made of the **seed of David according to the flesh**; and declared to be the Son of God with power...." **(Romans 1:3.4)**
- "He (Jesus) shall be great, and shall be called the Son of the Highest: and the Lord God shall **give unto Him the throne of His father David.**" **(Luke 1:32)**

Therein we see how the covenants had prophetic significance to the New Testament. We also noticed how the flow of God's plan progressed as He proposed it to happen from the beginning: "For precept must be upon precept, precept upon precept; line upon line, line upon line; here a little and there a little:" (Isaiah 28:10).

Chapter 18
The Revelation of the Trinity
(Part 2 - The Physical seed and the Spiritual Seed)

While it looks like we are dealing with two seeds, one for Abraham and one for David, in actuality, there is only one seed. Abraham's seed revealed as Christ in (Galatians 3:16) is the same as the one ascribed to David in (Romans 1:3). Perhaps a closer look at the two Scriptures might provide better clarification:

- "Now to Abraham and his seed were the promises made. He saith not, And to seeds, as of many; but as of one, **And to thy seed, which is Christ.**" **(Galatians 3:16)**

The verse states; to Abraham and his seed were the promises made. It goes on to mention, **"He saith not, And to seeds, as of many; but as of one...."** Because it is of *one seed* and not many, it indicates the passage is not referring to the Jewish people from which another promise occurred, but it relates to the physical attributes of Christ. In the following verse, we see the same seed as it relates to King David:

- "Concerning His Son Jesus Christ our Lord, which was made of the **seed of David** according to the flesh;" **(Romans 1:3)**

This passage *also* reflects the physical characteristics of Christ, but this time regarding the seed of David. Since there cannot be two physical seeds of Christ, the seed of Abraham is the same as the one attributed to David. The Bible ascribes Jesus' physical qualities to Mary, while His spiritual characteristics originate from God. From a spiritual perspective, the pure Seed is of the Holy Ghost. Although both seeds (the one of Abraham and David and the one implanted by the Holy Ghost) originate from different locations, they each meet at the same destination—the Virgin Mary.

The Genealogies:

Matthew and Luke's genealogies indicate they both belong to Jesus. Since bloodlines always go through the male, Matthew's gospel uses Joseph's line for the male sector even though God is the Father. However, due to the uniqueness of the Virgin Birth, the Bible lists both genealogies. The gospel of Matthew begins as follows:

- "The book of the generation of Jesus Christ, the son of David, the son of Abraham." **(Matthew 1:1)**

Matthew (1:2) begins the actual genealogy starting with Abraham instead of with Adam. The final verse covering the descendants (Verse 16) states that **Jacob begat Joseph,** the husband of Mary, of whom was born Jesus, who is called Christ. Therein we know this is Joseph's genealogy because it states outright that Jacob **begets** Joseph. However, Luke's gospel makes no mention of Mary in her genealogy since she is female. We understand this ancestry is of Mary because it names Jesus as the "supposed son of Joseph," meaning He was not the paternal father:

- "And Jesus Himself began to be about thirty years of age, being (**as was supposed**) the son of Joseph, which was the son of Heli." **(Luke 3:23)**

The Corrupted Seed:

In examining the natural seed, we find that even though Joseph's genealogy lists Abraham and David, it relates to Joseph's actual Jewish ancestry and not Christ's. Because Joseph had no input to Jesus' actual birth, we shall only deal with Mary's lineage. As shown earlier, Luke's gospel also associates Mary's genealogy with Abraham and David's seed. Seeing as her ancestry progresses from Adam, we need only trace things from where God initially promised Abraham. From there, we find it passes through a list of male receivers, and there is no need to confer the names of all the recipients. We are more interested in the final male individual who carries this particular seed, which turns out to be Mary's father, Heli (Luke 3:23). In tracking the genealogy further, Heli's daughter Mary becomes the last individual in the chain. Since Mary did not acquire the seed, as did the males, she became its by-product. Thus, she was the individual made from this seed, but solely to process the pure Seed.

Part 2 - The Physical seed and the Spiritual Seed

Everyone in Mary's genealogy, including Abraham and David, follow their lineage back to Adam. Mary's father, Heli, reveived the contaminated blood, meaning Mary also received a sin-nature. Because Mary was female and the seed's finality, it did not pass any further in her genealogy. Nevertheless, she did become the recipient of another seed—that of the woman (Genesis 3:15). Even though Abraham and King David's seed was not pure, it paved the way to bring God's Son into the world via a pure Seed through the Virgin Birth. It also provided the means for Jesus to belong to the human race. Thus, Abraham, David, and Heli's seed became the Virgin Mary, of whom God chose to bring His only begotten Son into the world.

Three Conditions:

Early on, we established that there were three requirements necessary to qualify an individual as a redeemer to reconcile humanity back to God:

1. The individual must belong to the human species, meaning angels and beasts were not eligible.
2. He must have no attachment to the blood of Adam.
3. He must live a sinless life with complete obedience to the Father.

Although the physical blood contains the sin-nature, we still must deal with it spiritually. That means, for the redeemer to meet the spiritual condition, He cannot have any contact with Adam's blood. To establish how Jesus complied with a Spiritual connection to God and a physical link to man, we must set Abraham and David's seed apart from the woman's Seed.

The Spiritual Bond:

The Spiritual relationship of Jesus to His heavenly Father originated from the prophesied Seed of the woman listed in (Genesis 3:15). Mary had yet to receive this promise from the Almighty until an angel appeared and announced that she would become the mother of the Son of God. When she agreed by stating, "Let it be done unto me according to thy word," it was then that "the power from on High" overshadowed her and the Holy Ghost implanted the pure Seed within her womb. At that instant, the pure Seed became the Seed of the woman. This setting confirms the (Genesis 3:15) prophecy but does not fulfill the second part of the verse regarding when the Seed bruises the serpent's head. That action occurred later at the Cross.

The miraculous overshadowing by the Holy Ghost occurred apart from an earthly father. In Mary's case, without any male intervention or an individual to wrap the genealogy around, the Seed automatically came under her custody. This also explains the omission of Mary's name under Jesus' lineage recorded in Luke's gospel. However, another matter confronted the pure Seed. It had to replicate the exact seed of a man by exhibiting the same characteristics.

A second condition mentioned previously stipulated that only a sinless individual without any connection to Adam's blood could qualify. It may help to reconsider at this time— the ovum (egg) of the female. It is infertile until inseminated by the male. The ovum does not contain blood, but once the male sperm introduces the blood at fertilization, life begins its process within the embryo. Throughout the infant's term in the womb, no blood-flow occurs from mother to baby or from baby to mother. In this case, the element introduced by the Holy Spirit produced the Blood and the Spiritual necessities for the Infant:

- "For unto which of the angels said He at any time, Thou art My Son, this day have I begotten Thee? And again, I will be to Him a Father, and He shall be to Me a Son." **(Hebrews 2:5)**

Adam's transgression blocked Mary's genealogical path from reaching God. Nevertheless, the Seed provided by the Holy Ghost united the Babe in her womb directly to God His Father. The Infant received His blood through the Father, meaning Mary's contaminated blood, which carried the sin-nature, did not invade the Fetus. Finally, we find that Jesus was faithful without sin throughout His life unto the cross, satisfying the third condition of the Redeemer.

The Physical Connection:

The chapter in this book about the Virgin Birth reported that the angel announced to Mary that she was to become the mother of Jesus. Mary was of the right family tree through her ancestry to David and Abraham. The betrothal period of her marriage to Joseph resulted in the precise time for her to receive conception by the Holy Ghost. She told the angel she had never known a man; therefore, carnal corruption did not occur. In another earlier chapter, we found that the mother supplies the physical necessities for the infant. Thus, Mary provided the developing fetus with the gene inheriting factors and other genetic provisions throughout the Child's growth in her womb. These necessities were essential to meet the Savior's qualifications to become part of the human race. From the physical perspective, Mary's actual ancestry from Adam, Abraham, and David to Heli qualified Jesus to develop as a Human Being.

When the Holy Ghost overshadowed the Virgin Mary, the fertilization process of the ovum took place in the manner of a standard conception. The pure Seed contained everything spiritually necessary (the Spirit of God, the Spirit of Jesus, His Soul, and the pure Blood). Although Jesus linked to Abraham through Mary's genetics, chromosomes, and other physical inheriting factors, He did not connect through the earthly matter called dust because He was not of the dust but a divine substance.

Jesus received Mary's hereditary factors to make Him Human and connect Him to David and Abraham. No corrupted blood passed from Adam to Jesus through Mary's lineage because the Seed's totality was from God. The sin-nature from Mary's blood did not invade the infant in her womb because from conception to actual birth, Mary's blood did not pass a single drop of blood to the Infant.

When Jesus made the statement, "I came down from heaven to do the will of My Father," it was because the *Seed* was *from* heaven.

Thus, Jesus connected to Abraham and David through the flesh using Mary's genealogy. There was no physical or spiritual connection to Adam in the pure Seed of the Holy Ghost. Because there was no human male involvement, it was **strictly through the genetic inheriting factors of the Virgin Birth itself and Mary's genealogical connection to King David and Abraham** that processed, developed, and transformed Jesus into a Human Being.

Now, let us look at what the substance of the pure Seed contains.

Chapter 19
The Revelation of the Trinity
(Part 3 - The Substance of the Pure Seed)

Most Christians and Church leaders classify the Trinity as a mystery that no one shall ever fully comprehend. However, God's Word declares just the opposite—that it would be revealed and made known (Matthew 10:26). The following two passages uphold this assessment:

- "Come ye near unto Me, hear ye this; **I have not spoken in secret from the beginning;...**" **(Isaiah 48:16)**
- "For there is nothing covered, that shall not be revealed; neither hid that shall not be known." **(Luke 12:2)**

Modern technology has opened up several Bible passages that seemed like mysteries in times past. Perhaps most notable is the account of the two witnesses lying in the streets of Jerusalem (Revelation 11:4-12). Without the invention of television, cell phones, and satellite, it would be impossible for the whole world to see them. Another incident occurring in Revelation regards everyone receiving a chip in the hand or forehead to buy or sell. That possibility could not happen without the computer. The Book of Daniel also declared that men would go to and fro at the time of the end, reflecting the increase in today's travel. The Book of Nahum had this to say thousands of years ago about travel:

- "The chariots shall rage in the streets, they shall justle one against another in the broad ways: they shall seem like torches, they shall run like the lightnings." **(Nahum 2:4)**

Many other concealed prophecies have transpired in our day, so it should come as no surprise that the Trinity is among them. This closing chapter will yield one more sample of evidence to fit the last puzzle piece into place.

Understanding the composition of the pure Seed is essential for connecting this concluding bit of the mystery. Because Jesus came forth directly from God, the pure Seed did not derive from dust, as with mortal man. Yet, it had to come into being from some type of matter. Therefore, what did the divine substance consist of, and what was its origin?

Genesis and John's Gospel:

The book of Genesis and John's Gospel begins with the exact three words: "In the beginning." Genesis 1:1 finds the Father creating the heavens and the earth. Verse 2 declares, "...the Spirit of God moved upon the face of the waters." In verse three, Jesus speaks the words, "Let there be light:" We find the Trinity displayed as the Father, the Holy Ghost, and the Son within the first three verses of Genesis. Keeping these details in mind, let us take a closer look at John's gospel. In reading the first chapter of John, the entire contents mention many specific details about Jesus Christ found nowhere else in the New Testament.

John reports the three words, "In the beginning," in a different way, yet the context remains the same:

- "In the beginning was the Word, and the Word was with God, and the Word was God. The same was in the beginning with God. **All things were made by Him**; and without Him was not any thing made that was made." **(John 1:1-3)**

Forwarding our reading of John's gospel to Verse 10, it states that "He (Jesus) was in the world, and the world was made by Him...." Our next verse to explore is listed in (John 1:14), which reads: "the Word was made flesh, and dwelt among us, (and we beheld His glory, as of the only begotten of the Father"). Progressing to verse 1:18, we come across something we may want to examine a little closer. Here we find a significant statement covering several essential details:

- "No man hath seen God at any time; the only begotten Son, which is in the bosom of the Father, He hath declared Him." **(John 1:18)**

When we break this verse down into more clearly defined details, it discloses that no man has ever seen the Father at any time. The next part of the verse enlightens us to where the only begotten Son is dwelling—***in* the bosom of the Father**. However, John's writings in this first chapter also point out that Jesus is dwelling on earth. For a better understanding, it might help to explain what the Bible classifies as a bosom. Its meaning is several things, including the belly, the heart, the spirit, the soul, or the midst of a being.

Several verses later in this first chapter, we find John the Baptist baptizing Jesus. Although John's gospel does not record where the Father is during Jesus' baptism, another passage (Matthew 3:16) does. The report shows that the Father is in heaven as the verse declares, "And lo **a voice from heaven**, saying, This is My beloved Son in whom I am well pleased." In comparing the two passages together (John 1:18 & Matthew 3:16), we find that at the exact time of Jesus' baptism on earth, He is also dwelling in the bosom of the Father, which was in heaven.

Now another matter arises, "How is it possible for the only begotten Son to be residing in the Father's bosom in heaven the entire time He is living upon the earth?" Scripture generally validates Scripture, so as we look for possible verification of this detail, we stumble upon a similar passage two chapters later in John's gospel. However, this time, instead of the apostle John writing about it, we find Jesus speaking this evidence Himself as He makes the following declaration:

- "And no man hath ascended up to heaven, but He that came down from heaven, even the Son of man **which is in heaven**." **(John 3:13)**

Jesus directs this passage to the Jewish ruler named Nicodemus as they both walked together upon the earth. He even mentioned that He (the Son of man) is in heaven while walking and talking with Nicodemus. Hence, we have practically the same state of affairs occurring in both passages. In one, Jesus is dwelling on earth while at the same time existing in the bosom of His Father. In the other, Jesus said He was in heaven, yet He was on earth talking to Nicodemus. Because these two passages seem to confirm one another, it now presents a different situation. Since the pure Seed is of a spiritual make-up, we want to determine what component spiritually occupies the bosom. A further page through the Scriptures leads to another passage in Matthew's gospel, where we discover Jesus making this statement:

- "...how can ye, being evil, speak good things? for out of the **abundance of the heart** the mouth speaketh." **(Matthew 12:34)**

Herein, Jesus forms an association of our heart to our words. He mentions that the words, which come out of our mouth, develop first in the heart. However, would this passage also refer to what God speaks coming from His heart?

Since man is the only creature made in God's image, we see many similarities between God and man throughout the Scriptures. We find that God has eyes, hands, a face, back parts, a mouth, and a voice among those likenesses. Other passages reveal God is laughing and that He is a jealous God. However, one striking resemblance to man that provides a helpful clue carries us to a passage that illustrates **the heart of God**; this time in association with something He said:

- "And the LORD smelled a sweet savor; and **the LORD said in His heart,** I will not again curse the ground any more for man's sake; for the imagination of man's heart is evil from his youth...." **(Genesis 8:21)**

This passage reveals that God has a heart and mentions what He said within His heart. Like the many other resemblances to man, the words God speaks comes from within *His* heart. Therefore, we must conclude that Jesus' statement, "...out of the abundance of the heart the mouth speaketh," pertains to both God and man. To distinguish where and how we delegate our words: the voice utters the words, the mouth vocalizes them, but the heart is where they originate. Therefore, we shall focus on the heart to answer the questions: What substance expresses the pure Seed, and from where did it originate?

When we think of Jesus as the Word of God, we generally see Him as conveying what God wanted us to know. Even though

He communicated those things to us, we need to keep in mind that the heart or bosom of the Father contains the words of God. Thus, an evaluation of what we have found reveals that the pure Seed, utilized by the Holy Ghost to impregnate the Virgin Mary, was the very Word of God. In addition, it originated within the bosom or heart of the Father.

In another passage from John's gospel, Jesus said that the words He was speaking were not His words, but those of the Father who sent Him:

- "He that loveth me not keepeth not my sayings: and **the Word which ye hear is not mine, but the Father's which sent Me.**" (John 14:24)

In another place, Jesus said, "**I have not spoken of Myself, but the Father which sent Me. He gave Me a commandment, what I say, and what I should speak.**" "**...whatsoever I speak therefore, even as the Father said unto Me, so I speak.**" These passages from (John 12:49.50) support that Jesus is the Word imparting messages to us from the Father, but also He is the literal Word of God. Thus, the Father birthed the words in His heart and delivered them through Jesus as He spoke them upon the earth.

The Word from Heaven:

Jesus stated, "For I came down from heaven, not to do mine own will, but the will of Him that sent Me" (John 6:38).

Jesus' purpose was to come down from heaven to do the will of the Father. Jesus had a definite objective to fulfill while He was upon this earth. Not only was He the Word (the pure Seed), but His body contained **the only source of pure Blood** anywhere in the world. He alone holds the key to redemption. Nowhere in the entire universe was there anyone else who could save us from an eternity of death, hell, and the grave. Those sins required payment in one way or another; God's Word declared it. **"The soul that sinneth, it shall die"** (Ezekiel 18:20). Yet, how was God able to put it all together? It was through the pure Seed, not a natural substance but a divine essence. The Holy Ghost implanted God's Word—the same Word contained within God's heart, and it became the Seed established within the Virgin Mary's womb. God was in heaven, but His Word was the Infant in the womb. Jesus was on the earth and also in the bosom of the Father.

The Word Always Existed:

Because God is from everlasting, it means that the Word of God is from everlasting. Life comes forth from God. When He spoke the worlds into existence, He used His Word. When God said in (Genesis 1:3), "...let there be light..." there was light. God employed His Word, "For He spake, and it was done..." (Psalm 33:9). The Word was Jesus in (Genesis 1:3), although not incarnate at the time. Thus, Jesus (the Word of God) always existed with the Father.

- "In the beginning was the Word, and the Word was with God and the Word was God." **(John 1:1)**

- "And the Word was made flesh, and dwelt among us,..." **(John 1:14)**

Body, Soul, and Spirit:

It may seem that Jesus did not have a Soul or choice of His own because he spoke the words and did His Father's will. From an earlier chapter, we gathered passages mentioning the Father having a Soul and a Spirit. For Jesus to become Man, He needed to be born with an earthly Body, Soul, and Spirit. The following passages attest that Jesus has a Soul, a Spirit, and His own will:

The first passage verifies Jesus has a Soul, but it also provides an answer to another question concerning corruption, "Did the sins that Jesus bore on the cross corrupt Him in any way?"

- "For Thou wilt not leave My **Soul** in hell; neither wilt Thou suffer Thine Holy One to see corruption." **(Psalm 16:10 & Acts 2:27)**

The following passage confirms that Jesus has a Spirit. It also validates (Ecclesiastes 12:7), which signifies at death, the spirit goes back to God who gave it:

- "And when Jesus had cried with a loud voice, He said, Father, **into Thine hands I commend My Spirit**: and having said this, He gave up the ghost." **(Luke 23:46)**

This remaining passage finds Jesus in the "Garden of Gethsemane." He just returned to prayer after telling His disciples that His soul was exceedingly sorrowful, even unto death. The passage confirms Jesus possesses His own will apart from that of His Father:

- "...and kneeled down, and prayed, Saying, Father, if Thou be willing, remove this cup from Me: nevertheless not **My will**, but Thine, be done." **(Luke 22:41.42)**

Born-again of Incorruptible Seed:

A passage from the epistle of Peter validates our findings by pointing out that the **incorruptible Seed** exhibits the **Word of God**. It reveals that Jesus was not born of Adam's corruptible seed but the Father's incorruptible Seed. In addition, it confirms that the Trinity was never a mystery. These answers were always in the Bible because Peter wrote and revealed it nearly 2000 years ago:

- "Being born again, **not** of corruptible seed (Adam), but of **incorruptible (Seed), by the Word of God,** which liveth and abideth for ever." **(1 Peter 1:23)**

The Lord God spoke this to Moses among the Israelites, " I will raise them up a Prophet from among their brethren, like unto thee, **and will put My words in His mouth;** and He shall speak unto them all that I shall command Him" (Deuteronomy 18:18).

Another event finds Jesus talking to His Apostles and mentioning that if you have seen Him, you have seen the Father. An Apostle named Philip answered and said to Him, "Lord, show us the Father, and it will suffice us." Jesus replied to Philip, "He that has seen Me has seen the Father" (John 14:8.9).

The Only Means for Redemption:

Jesus could not have fulfilled His position in the Father and accomplished His task as the Redeemer by any other means. Salvation required a spiritual connection, and only the Word of God could satisfy that purpose. It came **from the heart of God** and produced the incorruptible blood of the Lamb of God.

The Multitude of Answered Questions:

The Trinity has accumulated an abundance of questions over the years. The list below provides a sampling that covers some of those difficulties from times past. Note: the first sample on the list has puzzled many for ages:

- If Jesus is God, why does He not know the day or hour of His return? **(The Father has yet to speak it).** (Matthew 24:36)
- How is the LORD our God one LORD—yet manifested in the Trinity? (Deuteronomy 6:4)
- How could the apostles see the Father when they saw Jesus?" (John 14:11)
- Why did Jesus say, "All men should honour the Son, even as they honour the Father?" (John 5:23)
- How did Jesus become God's only begotten Son? (John 3:16)
- How can Jesus and the Father be one? (John 10:30)
- How can Jesus be in the Father and the Father in Him? (John 14:10)
- Was Jesus always God? (Genesis 1:3)

****

What the Word Does & What the Word Is:

What better substance could God have chosen for the pure Seed? Here is what the Bible says about the Word:

The Word is true. (Psalms 119:160)

The Word is truth. (John 17:17)

The Word is pure. (Proverbs 30:5)

The Word is perfect. (Psalm 19:7)

The Word keeps one from sin. (Psalms 119:11)

The Word can save. (James 1:21)

The Word sanctifies. (1 Timothy 4:5)

The Word is alive & powerful. (Hebrews 4:12)

The Word shall stand forever. (Isaiah 40:8)

The Word will never pass away. (Matthew 24:35)

The Word is food for our soul. (Deuteronomy 8:3)

The Word shall Judge. (John 12:48)

The Word is the power that framed the world. (Hebrews 11:3)

The Word is more desired than gold. (Psalms 19:10)

The Word dispels darkness. (John 1:5)

The Word is a lamp unto our feet. (Psalms 119:105)

****

Words Are Spiritual:

We tend to reject words as a means to impregnate a woman. From a physical prognosis, this outlook makes sense. Still, we must remember that words are a spiritual element; they originate from the heart. We can hear words but cannot see them. Our separation from God does not occur physically; it is the spiritual component needed for salvation. Any seed derived from a material basis would not meet the requirement.

The Transformation Process:

To fulfill His purpose of fellowshipping with someone like unto Himself, God chose dirt as the means. How is that possible? It is by way of transformation. As God changed dust into flesh, a follower of Jesus transforms from an old fleshly nature into a new spiritual creature. He becomes what the Bible calls a new creation in Christ. His flesh might go back to the dust, but his soul goes on to be with his Lord. Thus, he is no longer corruptible but changed into incorruptible (1 Corinthians 15:49.50).

Words As They Pertain To Man:

The Bible also has much to say about the words of man. There is something about the spoken word. It can be poison or a blessing; it can cause wars or make peace. The following passage illustrates what prowls around in our hearts:

- "...the imagination of man's heart *is* evil from his youth...." **(Genesis 8:21)**

Due to his sin-nature, man is capable of speaking evil things that defile him. The book of James reports that no man can tame the tongue. What we feel inside is what we speak, and what we say is how others perceived us. If we continually lie, we lose our trust. If we do not keep our word, it becomes worthless. The Bible discloses the potential of our words:

- "Not that which goeth into the mouth defileth a man; but that which cometh out of the mouth, this defileth a man." **(Matthew 15:11)**

Idle Words and the Judgment:

What Jesus reveals in the passage below about the words we speak makes what we say of even greater importance. Because words are spiritual, it discloses that they do not go to the grave with us but go on into eternity, kept in store until the Day of Judgment:

- "But I say unto you, That every idle word that men shall speak, they shall give account thereof in the day of judgment." **(Matthew 12:36)**

Words, the Vital Part of Man:

Since God made man in His image, and our words come out of the surplus of our heart, we must conclude that God's Words come from the abundance of His heart. That truth demonstrates how much God loves us. If someone ever said that God has a best part, we would have to conclude that He gave the very best part of Himself, straight from His Heart, as a sacrifice for our salvation. However, for everything He went through to purchase our redemption, He desires the very best part of us in return—that is, He wants *our* heart. In the following passage, Jesus answered one of the religious who asked, "What is the greatest commandment of all?" In response, Jesus recited the entire segment of (Deuteronomy 6:4.5) to the Jewish leader:

- "And Jesus answered him, The first of all the commandments is, Hear, O Israel; The Lord our God is one Lord: And **thou shalt love the Lord thy God with all thy heart**, and with all thy soul, and with all thy mind, and with all thy strength: this is the first commandment." **(Mark 12:29.30)**

****

Chapter 20
The Final Analysis

The Crux of the Cross:

Putting the divinity of Jesus and other such matters aside, the significant difference between Jesus and natural man is ***sin***. His primary purpose for coming to earth was to provide humanity a way out from sin's consequences. Yet, He did not sin but took upon Himself our sins instead. Jesus could not die physically because He did not acquire Adam's tainted blood. He could not die spiritually because He did not obtain Adam's sin-nature. So how was He to attain the feat of dying both physically and spiritually? That is, to die physically so His Body could rest in the tomb. To die spiritually so His Soul could receive our sins and deposit them in the lower reaches of the earth (Ephesians 4:9).

Sin occurs first in some manner of the flesh (physically), then manifests in the heart (spiritually). When Jesus took our sins, they had to penetrate His flesh and then enter His Soul. From an earlier chapter, we found that sin causes an immediate spiritual death due to a separation of God's Spirit from man's spirit. The spirit does not die, but the soul no longer receives radiating Life from the convergences of God with man. Consequently, Jesus' Spirit separated from the Father's Spirit in the same manner as happens with mortal man. As a result, (Ezekiel 18:20) "The soul that sinneth..." saw its fulfillment through Jesus on the cross. The following passage from Isaiah declares that the Father made His soul an offering for sin:

- "Yet it pleased the Lord (the Father) to bruise Him: He hath put Him to grief: when Thou shalt make **His Soul an offering for sin....**" **(Isaiah 53:10)**

Jesus endured sufferings through scourging, thorns, carrying the cross, and nails. He had just enough blood left in His Body to sustain Him until the exact time to receive our sins. When the time came that He was ready to expire physically, the Father would be prepared for Him to die spiritually. That incident would occur when the Father would place the world's sins upon the Soul of Jesus. While Jesus did not obtain a sin-nature, and His blood was void of any contaminates, the life of the flesh is still in the blood. Jesus was fashion as a Man even though His linage did not go back to Adam. However, He still needed blood in His body to sustain His flesh. As with mortal man, without a sufficient amount of blood in His system, He **could** die physically, even if free from sin's corrupting effects. Although He was totally God, He was also fully Man and subjected to God's laws concerning man.

- "Who, being in the form of God, thought it not robbery to be equal with God: But made Himself of no reputation, and took upon Him the form of a servant, and was **made in the likeness of men**: And being found **fashion as a man**, He humbled Himself, and became obedient unto death, even the death of the cross." **(Philippians 2:7.8)**

That moment was in the Father's hands, and like everything else in God's timing, it occurred as He proposed it to happen from the beginning. Jesus was at the point of physical death due to lack of blood. At the precise instant that His blood level reached the point of termination, the Father placed the sins of the world upon Him. It became the first time He was eligible to die. Those sins Jesus bore on the cross transferred to His Soul. This is where Jesus cried out, "My God, My God, why hast Thou forsaken Me?" Then again, Jesus cried out, "Father into Thy hands, I commend My Spirit." At that time, the separation of Jesus' Spirit from the Father's Spirit occurred. Thus, being fashioned in likeness as a man, He died both physically and spiritually.

Therein, He completed His mission on earth, but those sins could not merely remain on Him. The total penalty needed reparation. "Thou hast laid Me in the lowest pit, in darkness, in the deep—Thou hast put away Mine acquaintances far from Me…" (Psalms 88:6-8). Thus, He took those sins into the lowest hell and paid the penalty. Death could not hold Him, for He was an innocent Man. Recall the passage, "... Thou wilt not leave My Soul in hell..." (Acts 2:27). As a result, he recaptured the dominion authority and has the keys to death and hell (Revelation 1:18).

To answer the question, "Was the Trinity the mystery that many have concluded all these years?" No—God's timing was not ready, and technology was unavailable to the early Church. Even the Apostles who wrote the New Testament did not know the rest of the story. Indeed they were inspired to write enough given to them for their time. However, without today's knowledge, biblical understanding, and inspiration of the Holy Spirit, none of these disclosures would be possible. Since God's ways are unsearchable, we have barely scratched the surface regarding God and His Godhead. Perhaps a statement penned at the end of John's gospel best fits this perception:

- "And there are also many other things which Jesus did, the which, if they should be written every one, I suppose that even the world itself could not contain the books that should be written. Amen." **(John 21:25)**

Of all the things mentioned in this book, if there was ever a real mystery concerning the Trinity, it is this, "How could such a just and righteous God love sinful man as He does?"

At this point, we can look back and see what St. Patrick failed to observe in his shamrock analogy and what the Nicene Council missed in their attempted documentation of the Trinity. However, it was all in God's timing—precept upon precept.

Indeed the Palmist was right when he wrote, "The fool has said in his heart, there is no God." As mentioned, the Trinity and life are inseparable but available to all. Therefore, if you have never made Jesus your Lord, consider this time the first day of your eternal life. Jesus is the only pathway leading to salvation; make your commitment now. In conclusion:

- "The grace of **the Lord Jesus Christ**, and the love of **God (the Father)**, and the communion of **the Holy Ghost**, be with you all, Amen." **(2 Corinthians 13:14)**

www.ingramcontent.com/pod-product-compliance
Lightning Source LLC
LaVergne TN
LVHW022002060526
838200LV00003B/62